Pea Ridge Co-op

Shunryu Suzuki-Roshi

The Farm is a spiritual community owned and operated by the people. Stephen is our teacher.

PLENTY is our international non-profit charitable relief organization.

This book was put together by:

Publisher: Paul Mandelstein   *Editor:* Matthew McClure   *Art & Photography:* Mark Schlichting   Peter Hoyt   James Hartman   Alan Bishop   Nancy Leffer   Edith Lucas   Daniel Luna   David Frohman   Clifford Chappell   Valerie Epstein   Brian Hansen   Michael Jones   Lisa Griffin   Robert Tepper   *Composing:* Jane Johnson   John Pielaszczyk   *Lay Out:* Jimmy Egan   Katherine Nestler   *Lithography:* Jeffrey Clark   Jody Scheflin   Ivan Rijhoff   *Printing:* Robert Seidenspinner   John Seward   Alan Meltzer   Roger Spaulding   Andrew Nestler   Martin Reed   Brian Byrne

Volume One

Sunday Morning Services on The Farm

by

Stephen Gaskin

An Ongoing Search

An old European intellectual-type novel starts off with two people meeting in a train station—that sort of thing happens in European novels—and they look in each other's eyes, and one man, from looking in the other's eyes, can tell that the other fellow has seen a saint. Not that he *is* one, but that he has seen one. This is the first time in his life that anything like this has ever happened, and once he can tell that this person had seen a saint, the rest of the book is about his searching out everybody that other man ever met or ever knew, to find out *who*. He dropped everything—all his projects, all of his get-rich, or be-a-famous-writer-someday—everything, to find out which one, of the people that man knew in his whole life, which one of them was a saint.

There is an ongoing search for the Holy. Not only a search, but once you've had a taste of it, you have to have some more of it, and find out how to get closer to it. In the *Bible,* there are scores and scores of pages of things you're not supposed to do because they'll mess you up so you won't be able to find it: they

talk about *keeping the Sabbath*. There's a period of time during which you're not even supposed to make a fire. You're not supposed to take your mind off God, or searching for God, or something Holy, long enough to make a fire—which in those days, meant going through all the changes of flint and steel or fire by friction or something like that. That commandment is carried down into these days, even down to striking a match. And they say, if you find a fire that was going since yesterday, it's okay to get a little of it. In modern law, that includes hot water heaters, for instance; if the pilot on your hot water heater has been going since the middle of the week, it's cool. But the intention of all that was to don't be messing around doing something on the Sabbath other than finding out what is Holy, or following what is Holy: keeping the Sabbath.

When you come up to this meditation on a Sunday morning, you should start being quiet and getting your head together for a Holy frame of mind from about a quarter of a mile out, so you can bring a together head up into it, in respect for the flame of Holiness that is created by several hundred people trying to get through.

Sometimes you have to teach folks to do something. For instance, there is a question of praise and blame. I generally tell people not to praise each other. In the greater society it is considered that if anybody does anything, it's either for praise or for money, and it's considered polite to come up and really slop it on, really lay it on thick. I mean, it's okay to say, "Thank you. That was nice," but . . . Now about blame, although in general you're not supposed to go around unloading a lot of blame on one another; I don't usually teach about that much because that doesn't seem to be a useful teaching. A useful teaching seems to be: To be sure enough of what you're doing in your own heart that you're not going to be ruined, destroyed, devastated, or run off to tears because somebody doesn't like what you're doing. So I say, "Let the buyer beware,"—you just have to be strong and know what you're doing.

But in trying to raise your mind to a Holy place, the teaching is about how to not get distracted, how to let go of small and unimportant things, and let your mind rise to a high place. A lot of times on Sunday, I say we need to think about the greater welfare of the Farm. But if I'm sitting meditating on Sunday, and I find myself thinking about the greater welfare of the Farm, that's sort of the same as sitting there thinking about fixing the water truck, or something, because that's what I do all the time, and I just can't do that on a Sunday morning—I have to do something different from that. You have to let go

of everything that's going on. Don't be distracted. In San Francisco when we meditated in Sutro Park, I used to go down and tell people to turn off their motors in the parking lot; I used to do that stuff to the point, sometimes, that I hardly had time to meditate myself—and that was all right. That's why they have people like ushers in churches, somebody who says, "There's an empty place in the corner." Everybody can let their mind do a Holy thing—and there's somebody whose job it is to be sure that all the people are taken care of so they don't have to take their minds off of that for something small and petty.

The Farm gets you high, just by itself. The Farm gets you high, but you have to pay very close attention to it. It's not like the Farm gets you high like reefer does. When reefer gets you high, there's a buzz, and you can tell by the buzz, even if you didn't notice otherwise. That buzz that goes along with a high is like a carrier wave that may be determined by material plane senses. But there's something else in there—and the Farm gets you high that other way. Not necessarily a buzz, although sometimes there's a buzz. The Farm gets you high. And if it doesn't or if we don't pay good enough attention to do that, . . .

Once I was lying in bed and I heard something in my head, but I didn't really hear it. It wasn't something you hear, or that you see; but it was something happening in my head that was as loud as if somebody was shrieking by my head, or as if some-

body brought a motorcycle in the room and revved it up to about 8,000 and kept it there, but it was silent. There was something—wow!—in my head, just really loud, and I tried to understand it and there came another blast of it. In a little bit after that, our new baby started crying. He had tried for awhile to get it on with us first, and nobody paid any attention to him. Then he had to come on and make noise, because we were just too gross to notice. Well, I was noticing it; I just didn't know what it was. And I'm quite sure that there are mothers who find themselves right at the edge of desperation because they sense—wow!—"What is it? What is it?" Especially new mothers sometimes find themselves feeling, "I'm not doing it right," or "Oh, it's terrible," or something like that, instead of answering the phone.

I had this flu that has been going around, the one that a lot of people have noticed. Not much juice, as they say, headaches, stomach aches, fading in the middle of the day—all that kind of trip. But I knew I had that bug; so when I'd start fading in the middle of the day, I'd go home and rest for a while, and I knew that this thing was happening to me. But interestingly enough, all during the time when that flu was passing on the Farm, people kept calling me up with the same head problems. Like, oh, they're paranoid; oh, their old man don't love 'em; ah, the kids ain't doing it right; ain't got no friends, you know: can't get their job done, they need relativity. Well, after enough

of them hit, then I could see, well, lookie here, here's all these folks thinking with their stomachs!

The thing we're doing here, I am told by a veteran sociologist and political scientist, is impossible. This is a man with a lot of political experience—he's been working for the government for a long time, been in politics, run campaigns for Democrats now and then, really understands politics, and he says the thing we're doing here is impossible. He says, "Of course, I see it happening. This causes a certain amount of conflict." Well, if it's just the material plane happening, if it's just the beans, and just the dirt roads, and just the painting crew, and building nicer houses for other people than you get to live in yourself—we've built some very nice places off the Farm—or doing the farming and choosing the very best, shiniest and prettiest of your vegetables and taking them to Nashville: if it's just that, it *is* impossible. There's supposed to be this other thing—this miraculous thing—that we really care for one another, and that we really are going to take care of each other.

And in the same way that you can feel that loud telepathic noise coming from that new baby, there is a loud telepathic signal here. If you just be quiet for a while, you can feel it. And if you get too used to it and don't pay attention to it, it's like living by a waterfall. People who live by waterfalls don't hear them. We meet once a week and say, "Lookie here, we don't want to live by a waterfall and not hear it."

I'm just now getting to get into the fabric of the Farm enough after having been gone for a year and having been away on tour, to start feeling the flows of the Farm weather, the Farm mind changing. The last couple of days before Ina May had her baby, I was just bouncing from place to place all day long for a couple of days. Any time I heard about anything, anybody that was having a hard time, anybody that was being heavy on somebody else—everything I heard about, I chased it down, just immediately until I found some information on it. Some of it was rumor, some of it was real; I just chased it all down. And after a couple of days, the Farm started feeling very together. Then Ina May had her kid and I laid back for two days. I came back out and all of a sudden I just didn't know anybody again. I had to start over again.

There's a polite fiction—sort of an untruth—that I find myself trapped in when I'm on tour. And there's only one way out of it, to make it not be an untruth; there's only one thing that can happen to keep it so I'm not trapped out there in a lie. I keep saying, "The Farm runs fine without me, the Farm runs just fine without me. See? I'm out here, and they're making it." And I come back off the road, and I almost need a bulldozer, it gets so weedy.

The thing I do is not that complicated. A lot of it is keeping my head when folks put bummers on me. I don't believe folks' bummers; I just don't. If somebody comes up and puts a bummer on me, I just don't believe it. Partly because I just don't believe it; but also, just because professionally, it would be a hassle if I did. Suppose you came up to me and said, "Oh, man, I ain't getting it on with my old lady," and I said, "Oh, that's too bad. The divorce rate is going up in the United States, I don't know what we're going to do, all these couples just breaking up all over the place. Really, man, that's just too bad." Or you might come up and tell me, "I think I'm nuts." Suppose I just said, "Aahhhhhh! Get away from me! Don't brush it off on me!"

Some folks accidentally fall into what I do. They don't really mean to; they just take over some kind of job, that they think is just one of the Farm jobs—like they be housing person. So they find themselves with this-couple-can't-get-along-with-that-couple, or this-couple's-kids-are-driving-that-couple's-kids-nuts; and we-can't-stand-this-single-man, he's-just-all-up-in

14

our-thing. Or we-want-a-different-single-lady, can-we-trade-this-single-lady-in-for-another-single-lady? And suddenly they find themselves out in it, doing that thing.

To get me off the hook about that, everybody has to try as hard as they can to integrate the whole Farm all the time. The people who fall into those jobs find themselves a little responsible for the whole Farm. Clinic ladies, midwives, gate crew, people like that find themselves responsible for the Farm all of a sudden. Sometimes it just blows their mind, sometimes they just shriek and run when they discover what it really entails.

If you're responsible for the whole Farm, that means your day's work is not done if there is anybody on the Farm who is untaken care of, loose, no place to sleep, a little nutty. If there's one person on the Farm who isn't making it, you ain't done yet. You need to get plugged into them, or *have* somebody plug into them; you should get them a friend, get them covered; get them a place to sleep, get them something to eat. We are not done if there is one person who is uncovered.

A lot of folks work at their job and figure that because they're coming home from their job, they're done now, and they don't have to do anything. "How come my supper ain't ready? I was out in the fields today." Or, "Here, I've been working all day, and here's somebody in my house who needs some attention." Yes. Here's the thing about attention. (Some of you have heard me say this so many times that it's almost becoming like *Our Father* or *Hail Mary* or something like that.) *Attention is Energy.* When I first got really stoned, I didn't know about it. I had to discover for a long time that I had really good energy and really good attention. The way I discovered it was after a couple of years of people milking me, like they milk a rattlesnake. They take a little container with a rubber top on it, and they tease the rattlesnake into striking at it; and when he strikes at it, his fangs go inside the little rubber thing on top and he squirts his venom into the container. Well, people did that to me for a couple of years, and I didn't understand how come. It wasn't like a plot or anything; it was just that if I could get suckered into something like that, it would be juicier for them. A few people knew it and actually did it on purpose, and a lot of folks did it just by accident. So after I discovered that I had good attention—that I had really good energy, and that whatever I put my attention into is going to prosper—I tried to create a place to put my energy so it wouldn't just be wasted, so it wouldn't be dissipated.

For example, going to the movies is a funny thing. If you go to a movie that has some information in it, you learn something and that pays you for your attention. If you go to a movie that is just which cowboy gets to shoot which cowboy, and there isn't any learning or information in it, then you are taking your solid gold attention—which is capable of making fields grow and babies bloom and people get healthy and sane—and putting it on a piece of nylon cloth with nothing behind it but a brick wall, for a couple of hours at a time. Can you see what a trap that is?

I tried to do it with Monday Night Class. I said, "Okay, I'll collect these folks and this good information about how to work your mind, and I'll really put my attention into this thing." And I put my attention into it very faithfully. I never missed a meeting. That's what I always say when people ask how come I always got to sit in front of Monday Night Class. It's because I was the only one who was there every time.

I worked hard building that thing. Everybody I talked to— if I got a ticket, I'd end up telling the cop, "Well, I do this thing down on the beach at the Family Dog—you ought to come down some Monday night, man." Well, the thing that I built was like one of those little wind generators that lights a light-bulb and proves there's electricity. It wasn't running anything: it wasn't doing anything. It was just there, and folks said, "Wow, look at all the juice." Hippies would hitchhike up from Santa Cruz and say, "Wow, you got to come see the juice, man."

I'm still doing the same thing. Except now it's not so much an experimental model: it's not just hooked up to a light bulb to prove there's electricity. It's hooked up to the Farm and the Farm is hooked up with the world. It's changing the consciousness of the country. It is actually changing the consciousness of the world. That's what I really do. If I'm not doing that, I might as well take up macramé or needlepoint or something.

The reason they used to hire Wyatt Earp and all those cats to clean up a town was because some dude would come in and take a town. They used to call it treeing a town. Maybe one dude, maybe a whole herd, would come in just to take over a town. They'd ride up and down the main street, shooting out all the windows.

I would like to think that I could take somebody in the Gate who is having a hard time—who's fairly disturbed, fairly unhappy—and let them loose on the Farm without telling anybody—without saying, "Hey, watch this dude, he's a little hot," and that if he could walk down on the Farm and everyone would interact with him properly, it would heal him perfectly. If everybody was impeccable in their conduct with him, it would heal him just to come in and do it. It does it a little bit anyway, but not like it could—nothing like it could. And to the extent that that doesn't happen, it makes it so we're not that different from New York City.

Sometimes people say, "Hey, man, the thing about the Farm is you can't do your own thing. In New York City, you can do your own thing." You can do your own thing in New York City. You can lay right down in the doorway and die, and everybody will let you do it. They will walk by and figure it's none of their business. They will let you do your own thing, man. It's true—you can. If that's what you're into.

I keep telling people that I don't believe in a devil that comes up and shows you his horn and tails, because if he did that, you'd say, "Get thee behind me!" You wouldn't put up with it. But Harley Davidson has a motorcycle ad for 1200 Ego. For real. And I saw an ad on a big billboard with a picture of an airplane, and in the background is the Bahamas or something and a bunch of dancing girls on the beach and all that kind of thing. And it says, "Take an ego trip." It's saying, "Put your attention into this." "Watch this one, man, here's one for you to put your solid gold attention into." There's a poem by somebody that says the mosquito may be bloodthirsty, but he only takes his belly full. He doesn't put your blood in the bank.

The Christians weren't thrown to the lions to persecute the Christians: that was not the major purpose. The Christians were thrown to the lions to entertain the Romans. It was just a by-product that the Christians got persecuted. That wasn't what it was about. It was just a trip the Romans were on.

This place is like a sanctuary. There's always this thing, of how much of a sanctuary is it going to be. There was a time on the Old Farm when we had the gates closed for several months and I knew everybody on the Farm very deeply. We had no visitors. I knew where everybody was at. We didn't use motor vehicles on Sunday. I don't think it's going to be quite like that. We can't close the gates anymore. We don't *want* to close the gates anymore. We really want to have people come and see what's happening. If I'm the only one trying to hold up the standards, I'm going to try; even if I slip my clutch a little, I'm going to continue to try. But if everybody isn't ashamed to say what it is—compassionately, and with kindness, but not ashamed to say what it is that we're doing here: that this is a religious and Holy place and we're trying to maintain a high and exalted consciousness . . .

I was talking with someone last night, and he said, "You said you're so fancy." I said, "I didn't say I was so fancy." He said, "You wanted to help people." I said, "That ain't nothing unusual." He says, "You might mean it."

18

One time a Farm carpenter was going to build a house for some local people and he mis-estimated it. He mis-estimated it enough that we used up all the people's money and we didn't build them a house. Well, he went out and he worked in Nashville as a carpenter, for months, and he made that money himself, personally, the same way the people he was building that house for made *their* money—out on a job. He went out and worked until he made enough money to finish that house, the way we estimated we could, so we wouldn't burn those people.

They say that when Milarepa the Yogi was a young man, his mother got in a hassle with her brother over some land. So she told Milarepa to go and study some black magic with this guru who taught that kind of thing, and to come back and zap her brother for her and get her brother's land for her. So he went out and he studied all this black magic. And unbeknownst to him and unbeknownst to his teacher, he also was a very heavy dude, but nobody knew this at the time. So he went and he studied with this dark guru and he learned all these evil spells. And he came back and threw a curse down on this village where his uncle lived. It wasted all the crops, all the cattle, burned houses, had giant centipedes crawling through the streets—to the point where it scared him. And he went back to the teacher that he learned that from, who said, "I had no idea you were that heavy when I taught you that stuff; I wouldn't have taught you such dangerous stuff if I'd known you were so heavy. I haven't seen those spells work in fifty years." He says, "What you got to do is, you got us both so bad in the hole from all the damage you've done—you got us so behind the karmic eight-ball that you're going to have to take everything you own, and everything I own, and go find yourself a respectable teacher and get yourself *straight,* man, for both of our sakes, or we've both had it."

So he went out looking for a teacher, with all this evil guru's possessions with him to trade, to try to get them out of the hole. As he was going down the road; Marpa the Translator was out plowing his fields nearby. Suddenly Marpa had a vision. He saw a beautiful cup, like a container of grace—a chalice, like the Holy Grail. He saw this beautiful cup, but it was encrusted with this filth, much too dirty to drink from. And he was told in this vision that he was going to get this cup, and if he could get this cup cleaned up, that all mankind could have a drink out of it. About this time, Milarepa comes boppin' down the road, filthy with bad karma. And Marpa took him in.

"Will you be my guru?" asked Milarepa.

And Marpa said, "Sure, I'm going to straighten you, boy." Then he said, "The first thing I want you to do is to go out and build me a stone house, oh, about fifteen feet tall and about fifteen feet square. Just build it of nice big stones. I'd like the stones about two feet square. And I'd like you to do this yourself."

So Milarepa went out and got these stones out of the ground and he built this great big stone house. And his teacher comes out and says, "Oh, too bad. I must have made a mistake. You built it on the property line. This is not my property, this is my friend's property. You'll have to tear this house down and move it back over the property line and build it over here."

So he tears the house down. His fingers haven't healed from all the times he banged his hands doing it last time, and he's at it again tearing this place down, carting the rocks across the property lines, putting it back up, taking quite a while. And Marpa comes out and says, "You dope, I didn't tell you there, that's my neighbor's land, you have to put it over here." And he says, "While you're at it, make it two stories."

So he did this to him eight times and each time the house got bigger. And bigger, until it was a mansion. And it was taking years and years. And Milarepa was getting scabby and hungry and sore and tired. He'd get half a bowl of rice a day, and he was building these stone houses on that. And then he had to tear them down. And on the last one Marpa said, "Oh, you're such a bad mason, such an incredibly worthless student! What I want you to do is tear that house down and put all those stones back in the ground where you quarried them and forget the whole thing." So he tore the house down, and took all the stones back to the quarry and put them all back where he got them, and about this time, Marpa the Translator's wife said, "Hey, what are you trying to do to this student? Look at him! He weighs about seventy-nine pounds. He's about three-quarters nuts! What in the world are you trying to do to him?" And she begged and begged: "Just give him a break."

But Marpa wasn't done yet. He told his wife, "Look, I was trying to do a thing. You may have blown it, but maybe it's all right. We'll try it out and see. What I figured was that, according to the amount of disaster that this man has brought on his fellow man, I had to plunge him to the depth of despair nine times—to purify his soul enough that he'd be clean in his heart again. Maybe you have blown it. We've done it eight times and the scene is kind of blown. He knows what I'm doing now. Since we can't really do it again, we'll try it like this and see if it'll work."

So they tried to see if it would work. And Marpa started a line of teachers. And Milarepa and all the entire tradition comes down from that line for all these thousands of years, because Marpa knew what he had to do, and he plunged his student to the depths of despair eight times.

I just wanted you to know what was going on here and not to think it was an old beatniks' home.

Now that feels like a good stoned place right there. It feels like you can remember how we are supposed to be together, and do it again for a week . . . I'll see you later on. God Bless you. Good morning.

August 24, 1975

Energy Amphibians

I was reading in a Buddhist book this week about the benefits that accrue to you if you ever get it together. It's sort of like trying to sell it to you, I suppose—"This is why you should do it,"—but I was so truly grateful to read one of them that I thought I should share it with you. It is, *To not be distracted by any doctrines or any dogmas.* Let's think about that for a minute, because there's so much scoop blowing around this planet right now, so many people saying they know where it's at; not only do they say they know where it's at, but they claim to have it exclusively.

To not be distracted by doctrines and dogmas. A man came to the Gate, who said he had flown all the way from San Francisco to ask me a question. He said there were these people out on the coast who say they are from another dimension, and that they are going to come back to life in front of everybody, and he says, "What are we going to do about this? They really are going to do this." This man was so disturbed by that doctrine that he had to get on an airplane from San Francisco and fly here and ask that.

And I said, "Man, talk is so cheap."

And he said, "What if they do it? What if they do it?"

"The entire scene is such a bad vibes and dark arts scene, that I don't care if they *can* do it," I said. It's similar to being told that Maharaj-ji is going to levitate down in the Astrodome or something like that—I didn't have to go see if it would happen or not; I didn't care if it did. I think some of knowing where it's at, is knowing where it *ought* to be at—if God was God at all, in any way just—which is almost as good as knowing where it's at.

Somebody was talking about being a bhakti yogi. And it occurred to me that being a bhakti yogi is like being a podiatrist, or an eye-ear-nose-and-throat man. Picking out any kind of yoga and thinking that's where it's at, is like trying to be a specialist of some kind. There are incredible complexities of religious teachings and structures that are loosed out onto the world. The only reason it looks like there are so many of them is that they are being taught by a bunch of specialists. And that's how you get the idea that you can't make it without the right mantra, or the right way to sit. They're specialists and they have a particular trip that they run through. But that's just almost forgetting what the *whole* trip is about, which is to become a complete generalist. Different kinds of energies come from different levels in us, and *all* levels have to be open.

I want to make a clear and more coherent teaching about energy. Someone's always saying, "Tell me how to get the energy up." But that's what we do: we have this real loose collection of different kinds of things, ranging from head trips like not being attached and stuff you do with your mind, meditation; stuff you do with your mind and your body, farming, yogas, how you talk to people, knowing how to open and close a meeting.

The energy is up, and it's getting higher. And as Buckminster Fuller says, "The better you get at solving problems, the worse problems you're going to get." We used to have to worry about the logging company and the land next door, and now we have to figure out about the oil-producing nations' combined price effect on the energy situation. But I'd like to get your help in really formulating how we are about energy, in ways that we can explain to folks, so that it doesn't seem strange to them.

There is an energy language on the Farm. I want you to be really careful and see if you can make a good raja yoga distinction between Farm Jargon and energy language. In your best good intelligence, start paying attention. Do you say it just because it sounds neat, or does it really mean something? Try to know what it is that you mean. I have had people come up and say paragraphs to me in Farm Jargon that I didn't understand any more than if it were some foreign language that I'd never studied: "What in the world are you talking about?" But I've had other people come up to me and lay out a paragraph that was equally as incomprehensible-sounding, by way of strange language, that was so accurate and so concise, and described a series of mental and energy relationships so accurately that I knew exactly what they were talking about; and I didn't know any other language that they could have told it to me in.

And that is really precious, because we are the energy amphibians; we live in the physical world and we live in the energy world, and we like both of them and don't want to quit. We don't want our physical world to run us down so much that we can't see the energy world; and we don't want to have to check out of living in the real world, either.

When we left San Francisco, we'd all been hanging out for five years rapping all this religion and energy rap to each other. And now we've been through some long changes, and the people who came here with me are in the minority. And a lot of people brought an energy language here. They'd studied somewhere and learned something; maybe just the people they'd tripped with had worked out a little bit; or maybe they'd actually studied with a teacher. But we have a combined thing here, that makes us a cultural resource and a treasure. We are like some sourdough starter, and some people want some. If folks want sourdough starter, it should sour dough.

And that's the real seriousness, for each one of you to get outside yourself. When I'm reading the *Diamond Sutra* sometimes, I look at it and I know a lot of people who would get uptight at this line right here: *No Bodhisattva who is a real Bodhisattva cherishes any idea of a separated individuality whatsoever.* Now that's a strong doctrine. But some people are going to look at that and say, "Oh, they're going to get all our heads; you're after our gourds, that's what you're after." But we have granted to us, by the three-dimensionality of the plane that we live in, a certain amount of separated *individuality.* We have separate bodies and separate fingerprints: we have a certain amount of individuality. But not only does a Bodhisattva not *cherish* individuality; it also says that no Bodhisattva that is a real Bodhisattva has any *concept* or *idea* of individuality whatsoever—*because on the conceptual or idea level, we are not in fact individual.* We are individuals with separate fingerprints and separate genes, but on the high planes, the spiritual planes and the mental planes, we are not in fact separate. And no Bodhisattva who is a real Bodhisattva cherishes any idea or concept of a separated individuality whatsoever, because the very act of cherishing such a concept

25

tends to estrange you from your fellow man, and tends to estrange you from God. So you don't mess around with concepts of individuality; you be who you individually and uniquely are. You can't be anybody else, anyway. It's the only game in town.

The stuff that's right at the threshold of your consciousness is very important, because that is where you run trips like, somebody saying something that doesn't make any sense at all, but seeming to be very intent about doing it—and you discover that the talking part is to keep you occupied while they do a piece of magic on you. And the less sense the talking makes, the more of their attention they have into what they are doing to you. Isn't that interesting? The more nonsense it is the more they are doing it to you, because the less of their attention are they able to afford to put into putting up good stuff for you to listen to, while they do it to you. That's one of those phenomena right around the threshold of consciousness.

Also, sometimes people make ego agreements at that threshold level. For example, when it comes to a heavy place and somebody looks around and says, "This is kind of heavy; I don't know if I can make it." And somebody winks that back at them and says, "Don't worry, we'll just cover it up and let it go," that's an ego agreement. And you can bury heavy stuff like that. And stuff that gets buried like that can get to be such a strong determiner in your consciousness, that you hardly have any freedom, from being so determined.

We have as a culture de-emphasized vision and dance as a communications medium. Vision and dance are a pair together: we dance for each other, and we look at each other dance. And some folks don't dance very well. But when folks really dance for each other, they can express things like their friendship and affection in a subtle dance from fifty feet away before they ever get close enough to talk to each other. When they get close enough to talk, they might say, "I ought to shoot you," but they've been saying, "I love you" for fifty feet with their body on the way. Those communications take place right at the threshold of consciousness, where sometimes somebody says something to you and you have to check again to see if they really meant that, because it's so subtle that you have to say it two or three times before I know what you mean. I believe in making your subconscious conscious: it makes you free.

The three hardest yogas I think are Brahmacharya, House-holder, and really being non-attached to the fruits of your labors. Brahmacharya is the yoga of absolute celibacy, which is one of the hardest ones—we see people falling off of it now and then, making loud splashes when they do. The house-holder yogi is responsible for raising a family. And the third one is really being in community and being non-attached to the fruits of your labors. There is probably one single Sanskrit word for not-accepting-pay-for-the-fruits-of-your-labor, and to-work-for-what-needs-done-and-what-needs-taking-care-of.

But that is a yoga in itself, the yoga of real community, a social *sadhana*. We can make that happen, out of a confidence and joy, and an awareness that you must never underestimate your ability to help other people, no matter how small you are. Our whole lifestyle is living close together, and not having very much and sharing it—sharing fortunes together—and all of that is a good yoga in itself.

Good morning. God Bless you.

December 26, 1976

Hippie Espontaneos

You know, we're pretty big. Sometimes I think the most important thing we can do is to try to keep our naturals together. I remember when we had such a small troupe with such a level of agreement that you could just close the Gate for about a week and pretty soon you'd know everybody on the Farm. Well, it takes a little longer than that these days; and we can't close the Gate, anyhow.

I was paying attention to the meditation this morning. It looked like about eighty percent of the folks knew what to do and were doing it; and a lot of other folks were cleaning their toenails, sunbathing, waiting for the OM, all that kind of thing.

The only way this thing we're doing can work, is if it's what we want to do, and if it's what we are doing on purpose because we want to do it. And any time we forget that, it's kind of a dusty condominium, not very well landscaped yet.

Some of the highest and most enlightened understanding of our practice is to make sure that we truly share fortunes, right down to the level of how much sugar and margarine there is, or the tin roof: that we truly share fortunes.

When I'm out on the road, I tell them how we live together and how we take care of each other medically and how we always research to be sure our diet's cool, and try to cooperate to take care of the kids, and share in our labor, and all that kind of stuff. And then, after I've talked about stuff like that for about an hour and a half, they say, "Well, would you tell us about your religion?"

Because I haven't mentioned anything out-front impossible, they assume I am not talking about religion yet. That's their definition of it: those things which are out-front impossible, which you don't have to pay any attention to, and something not to be mixed up with the business of making a living. Right?

I think a certain number of folks have two levels of behavior— one they give someone they think is "important," and another level of behavior for folks they don't think count. And it doesn't take much of that to make a subtle discipline like ours start coming apart at the seams.

We're based on trust. Now, some people think I expect a *really high* level of integrated trust among folks—they think it's almost inhuman for folks to be that caring and trusting of one another. But I'm not expecting anything more of the human animal than I see he can already do if he wants to—to get a beer, or get a big apartment: the levels of excellence and expertise that people attain purely for money are phenomenal.

If you really consider it, the only thing that keeps there from being broken automobiles littering the highways every twenty feet for millions and millions of miles across the United States, is a level of agreement, where people say, "Well, I won't pass on blind corners. There might be somebody coming the other way. Get me and him both in it, y'know?" We've all come here from somewhere else—logged thousands and thousands of miles out on that highway. Have you ever considered the hundreds of thousands of people you have met going the other way who had to not make a mistake for you to be here? How many millions and millions of people have you entrusted your life to, as strangers, with no more guarantee of their behavior than the idea that they may have a driver's license? Every one of them that comes past you may have been driving eight, ten, twelve hours, and all he has to do is space out for just a couple of seconds; and to a really amazing degree, he doesn't make a mistake.

In putting this together as a discipline, I try to avoid the trap of attainment. I don't like to see a bunch of folks running on a treadmill, chasing a carrot. I try not to put in any idea of attainment, or *"Then* he'll be cool." It isn't particularly profitable to divide us up into those who are cool and those who aren't, inasmuch as we're going to keep all of us anyway.

I've been gone quite a bit in the last six weeks. I think I've been on the road four out of six. And I get vibes from folks on the Farm sometimes, they say, "You got to spend more time on the Farm, get the Farm together; we need you," and all that, "You got to spend some time here." And about the most persistent question that I get on the road is, am I teaching you how to take care of yourselves, or are you dependent on me? Now, what should I do about that?

This country has a great deal of conditioning to not let the amateurs get into the action: they have this thing about professional qualifications. But the professional qualifications in many instances are just so much non-sense. In Mexico, they talk about the *espontaneos*. That's Spanish for "the spontaneous ones." And the *espontaneo* is the dude who's watching the bullfight, and he can't stand it any longer, and he jumps the fence into the bullring and whips off his suitcoat, and does a couple of passes with his suitcoat, *whhhhhsssss*. Until the bull gets him, or the security police get him, whichever first. That's the *espontaneo*. And there are people who don't even care about the man in the suit of lights. They dig the *espontaneos*.

Well, that's what we are. Out here, in this spiritual and political arena of the United States, we are a bunch of *espontaneos*. With our hippie coats on—going to whip them off and cape this bull. And if you thought you were a passenger, be careful. The bull might get you.

If you miss me or get shakey when I go off the Farm, then you aren't using me right. If you're using me right, you ought to be able to say, "Look what he gets away with. I wonder if I can get away with that," and step out a little. Somebody has to step out. If *somebody* doesn't step out, . . .

Sometimes there is stuff going down that isn't cool, and people will see it and not say anything about it, and let situations develop until they get really nutty. And then when they get really nutty, it becomes a question not of what a household can handle anymore, but of having to call the Gate crew or the midwives to come pull the chestnuts out of the fire. But nothing has to get that out of hand if you take care of it when it's still in its beginning stage. What it takes to take care of a situation when it's in its beginning stage is that kind of courage which you ought to cultivate like it was a rare and strange grass plant. You ought to think it isn't *at all* weird, or funny, or sentimental to think, "Well, *I'll* be Mighty Mouse." It doesn't matter if it's corny, if it gets the rent paid.

Somebody sent me a watercolor-drawn letter, wanting to come live on the Farm. She said someone had told her that the Farm really shapes you up like boot camp. And she had drawn this cartoon of a bunch of people standing in a row in bib-tops, with a lady walking up and down in front, saying, "All right. You babies get them jeans faded or we'll ship you back to Berkeley!"

It's a question of dedication. This is not a passenger ship. This is all crew. Everybody on here is crew. And you're welcome as crew. But you have to understand that it is as crew, because we don't have any passengers. That's what the commitment thing is about.

Every time I get into one of those long complicated things about how to do it, it comes down to the real simple ones like, "Love your God with all your heart and soul, and love your neighbor as yourself. This shall be the whole of the law."

Good morning. God Bless you.

June 13, 1976

31

There's two schools of thought about how we're doing what we're doing here. One of them is that we somehow need more rules to get more organized. This is sort of a weekday kind of thought, but the idea on Sunday is always to me that if you *really* understand what we're doing and you really know where it's at, then *all* the rest of it is a breeze, and all the stuff that goes on during the week is like a game—just so you don't forget and take it too seriously. You're supposed to take it seriously enough to do your very best work, and in the words of a great Japanese Zen Master, Suzuki Roshi,

"Don't goof off."

The thing that we're doing is getting so big that I've been telling people for a long time, "Watch closely what I do, because anything I do now, you may have to do next year." You just don't know how fast it gets. One of the things that is a spiritual discipline here that might not necessarily be a spiritual discipline anywhere else (although I think it's a spiritual discipline anywhere it appears, actually) is the necessity of the people to learn enough about how things happen and how things are governed in order that if you find yourself catapulted into a position of power and authority that you have enough morals and enough sense to don't immediately fall for the first ten dumb things you can do from that position.

I get rumors that we have a pretty dedicated store man. He really wants to do that thing, and I dig for him to do it. But at the same time, I get a rumor once in a while that a good-looking lady gets an extra cup of sugar. (Laughter.) This is one of the earliest abuses of power one can fall into. You see where it leads, of course. It takes hardly any time at all to get into Watergate. Plus, if you get all those ladies fat that attract your eye, what's it going to be like? On a level, that's just so understandable and so normal; that's why we all laugh. And at the same time, this is the very level where everyone who has a piece of the action hs to be so on-deck and take responsibility on themselves, personally, to keep it fair and just. If this is going to be a spiritual community it has to be fair and just first, or it can't be a spiritual community. That's a question the individuals have to take care of themselves.

Just because we don't have money among ourselves on the Farm, or just because we're on vows of poverty, doesn't mean that there aren't ways that payoff can happen. That means that you have to be alert enough to decide what is bribery in any language it is offered, or what is a fair way of using resources, considering that we're more than a thousand of us. I could talk about that for a long time, but what it really gets down to is that you already know what's fair.

(Q.: How do you get to having a sense of humor?) Well, one of the ways you get to having a sense of humor is to don't take yourself too seriously. A lot of people's sense of humor is reversed. They laugh when someone else slips on a banana peel, but not when they do. You're supposed to laugh when *you* slip on a banana peel, and *not* when someone else does.

(Q.: While I'm sitting here meditating, I'm wondering what am I supposed to be thinking about?) It's not so much a question of what you think about, as that *certain changes happen in your consciousness from just doing that thing.* This morning, when I first sat down, there was already a pretty strong thing happening here. There were probably a hundred and fifty people already before I got here. As soon as I entered

that, I could feel it. And I could feel I was with a bunch of people who already had it on pretty good. But I still had my head full of thoughts. So I went through a whole bunch of thoughts in my head. For a while, I went through a place where I said, "Well, I'm not going to just let all this garbage in my head keep me from doing this thing," so I kind of dismissed all that and started doing stuff with my attention just to get myself together, like listening to the wind for a while, or picking out a cricket that's way back there and hard to focus on, and listen to him for a while. That cleared away a certain level of stuff.

Then I had some things so insistent that I had to keep thinking about them. A thing's been going on now with someone on the Farm where we're having a discussion about how strong to make something to move something big, and he thinks that we're rival engineers; and I don't think we're rival engineers, I think I'm the Department of Safety. He feels like that I'm messing in his thing, that maybe I don't know everything I ought to know. So I had to think about that because that's a heavy trip.

That went through my head for a while and then I said, "Well, I don't have to do anything about it in particular right this minute, all I know is that as the changes go down the line, I'm going to be there and make sure that it happens right. And if I really make an agreement with myself, I'm going to be there and not let it go down any way that isn't right, then I can quit thinking about it now and let that go. I don't have to worry about that now." Well, if you make an agreement with yourself that you keep, and you really do follow up afterwards and you take care of these things, then you'll build enough good credit with yourself that when you tell yourself while you're meditating that "I don't want to do this right now, I want to get high, I don't want to bother with this level of thing, I'll take care of it when I get to it, for real," then you'll just believe yourself and just go ahead and go on up.

After a while, if you keep doing that, so much stuff will pass through your mind, in many different directions: one minute your observer will be watching you listen to the wind, and the next minute your observer will be watching you thinking about your troubles, and the next minute your observer will be watching the skyline, and the next minute your observer will be noticing that it's warm, and pretty soon your observer notices itself—"Oh! Look, there's one piece in there that doesn't move. All the rest of that stuff has been flopping and flipping around and going through all those changes, and there's one piece that didn't move. Far out, look at that." And then you be that. Solid, like a rock, just be that. Sometimes you forget that, and that's why you meditate now and then, is to go back to it and remember it again.

The thing about the cup of sugar to a pretty lady—it doesn't already presuppose that we already love each other. We already love each other from in front. The love in that cup of sugar was expressed by the carpenter who banged the nails enough to buy that cup of sugar, and by whoever bought the gas that brought it to the Farm. That's the love that's expressed in that cup of sugar right there. It doesn't need any further expression of somebody special, it's already been expressed as a loving gift.

Every time you have a glass of soy milk, or a piece of soy cheese or tofu, it's a loving gift from someone who was not paid, and did it out of their heart . . . never going to make money for it. Every time you eat a slice of bread ground out of our wheatberries—there's a lot of stuff we do for each other here, and all of that stuff we do for each other we have to recognize as an expression of love. That is, in effect, the meaning of the transaction: it's an expression of love rather than commerce.

I think I might let us loose around in here, and I'm very happy to be here this morning. It feels pretty smart here. God Bless you, and good morning. I'll see you during the week.

March 21, 1976

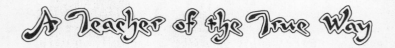

A Teacher of the True Way

In the teachings of Tibetan yoga, they have a saying that adversity, being a teacher of the true way and likely to turn one toward a spiritual life, is not necessarily to be avoided.

I think I know what that means and how it relates to us. We're doing two or three different things here. One of them is running this Farm; one of them is whatever we have to do to get along together, and then there's the idea that we're all going to be growing and maturing and fulfilling our potential and branching out and taking bigger pieces of the action and all that kind of thing—growing up. One of the things that I do, my whole household does, is get calls about people living with each other. There's something I've come up with a couple of times that people have just accepted so readily that I realized it was because they'd never thought of it; it wasn't because they were against it or anything, but they'd just never thought of it that way. They say so-and-so is a hassle and all that, and they say they want to kick them out, they want to get this hassle out of their thing. And I tell them, "No, no, we aren't trying to get this hassle out of our thing. What we're trying to do is get the hassle out of this person." We want to keep the person, but we don't want to keep the hassle. A little hassle is cool, because that's like having the grain come up so you can sand it a little, so you can see what's really going on. Because of things like necessity and having to work together and having to get these crops in and stuff like that, once in a while we have to say, "Well, that's too petty to do anything about right now. We have to move the tractor. We have to do this thing." But then sometimes you come to a place where you say, "Well, we have to do this for a little while."

It seems that the Universe is made of positives and negatives, about half each, and it seems that if you're going to taste anything very high and very fine, you have to have the nerve, which probably came to you from having tasted something that was heavy or hard to handle or hard on you or hard to accept, that you had to learn to accept. That's what gave you strength of character to get to the other place.

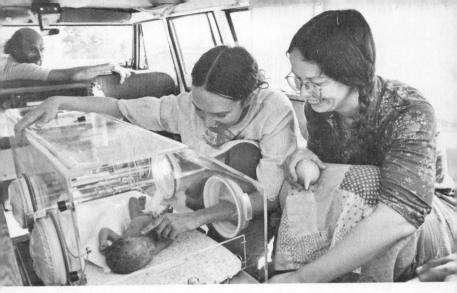

There are several kinds of healing energy. Everything we're doing here is a healing practice. If somebody comes here and just does the thing, it's going to change them. It's designed to do that. It's supposed to slow you down from your road speed and big-city speed and it's supposed to get you into more contact with where stuff really comes from so that you're more at peace in the world. It's a yoga, and it's healing. It's all healing as an overall Gestalt: fresh air, good food, good company, good thoughts and something important to do that's worthwhile doing.

Then there's laying on of hands, which is to transmit your healing energy with love. They do Kirlian photography these days where they take photographs of auras coming off your fingertips when you're stoned and when you aren't stoned, and when you're mad and when you aren't mad, and when you're sick and so on, and they're all different. You can put your hands on somebody and love them and want to help them. Sometimes I find myself thinking about somebody on the Farm who has some kind of problem and I'll think, "Boy, I wish I knew what to do about them," and then after thinking that for a while, I'll say, "Oh, I've been praying for them,"—not noticing it until getting caught in the act of it. If you've really got your attention riveted and intense and heavy and you're pouring it out in a certain place, it's healing.

Somebody asked me a question the other day about nick-names and handles and whole names—they had heard I preferred whole names. I do, but not as a rigid thing. There's a lot of fun in folk poetry and there are teachings in the flow of what kind of handles people have. I don't really mind that. It would be stiff and foolish to be formal all the time; but sometimes you have to look somebody in the eye and call them by their whole name. Now and then, just to let them know you know. And that's healing.

There's laying on of hands, and then there's making love, which is laying on of everything you have. Very strong. Our midwife practice is really a healing art. The midwives do other kinds of healing too—they're the mainstay of our clinic crew. When we had that heavy flu come through here, we spent a thousand dollars on the newest, fanciest, just-discovered African scrape-the-bark-off-a-tree wonder drug, because it was appropriate to the flu we had. We had people with that bug who were very young and very old and we didn't lose anybody, and it's because of our general atmosphere of healing and spiritual living. Sometimes there are specific exercises and specific yogas for people, but in general I think that you should make your yogas be something in your lifestyle that you just do as you go along.

We are profoundly affected by our surroundings. It's not a mystery to be affected that way. There are actual vibrations that do things to you. Your body is a semi-hard jelly. Its technical name is a colloid solution. Quicksand and silly putty are colloid solutions. So is protoplasm. Colloid solutions get harder or softer depending on what you do to them. If you hit silly putty with a hammer, it goes rigid and breaks up. If you leave it alone, it runs into a puddle. The stuff you're made out of is like that, too, and in the city, you're subjected to a constant series of physical and psychic shocks, just hitting on you all the time. Somebody on the other side of the block is getting mugged and putting out just incredible stuff and it's too far away for you to hear it, but it isn't too far away to feel the vibes. Vibes go a real long way. You're getting hit with stuff like that all the time when you're in the city. I used to live fourth house down from a traffic light, and my life was ordered by the traffic light for several years. Brrrrmmmmm! It was a one-way street up a hill, and they had this drag race past my house every two and a quarter minutes. It's a heavy trip living in the city. I had this pad that was five floors up and there was nothing across the street from it. I was sitting there and I became conscious of this roar and I thought, "What in the world is this sound? A flying saucer or something?" I finally realized it was just the sound of the city. It was early in the morning and it wasn't even heavy yet, it was pretty quiet, but there was this roar, this mighty roar coming on all the time. And San Francisco isn't that heavy. You get out into the middle of Chicago or New York City and GRRRR! the ground shakes under your feet. Monkey wants to hold on to a tree.

I think when Jesus said the thing about to neither sow nor reap but be like the little creatures which are fed by God, he meant to not sow or reap karmically—to don't create karma but to try to bring it to rest. It also says in the Book that God gave us every seed and every tree bearing fruit and every plant, and it shall be for us as meat. So we're instructed to till the earth and take care of ourselves.

(Q.: What are some of the ways that people come to know they have free will?) There was a fellow who was sweeping in his garden and the broom hit a rock and sent it over and it hit a little piece of bamboo and it went *ping!* and he said, "Oh," and he understood everything. Then there was a fellow who went in and was asking the Zen Master some kind of petty Mickey Mouse question that was really designed to show off what he knew instead of being a question that he wanted an answer to, and in the process of getting thrown out of the *dokusan* and having the door slammed on his leg, he came to realization. I know someone who had a heavy realization from taking a whole bunch of weird dope—he went into a fantasy trip where he suddenly saw that his apartment was on fire, and he opened up the door to the hallway and it was all flames outside. He ran over to the window, and was standing on the edge of the window looking out when that hallucination quit and there weren't any flames or fire or fire engine or net down there or anything. And he said, "Oh," and stepped back inside. It wasn't a full realization, but it was enough at the time.

(Question.) About self-confidence? *Con-* in confidence is *with*, and *-fide-* is *faith* and it means *with-faithness*. Having confidence is having good faith. There's a teaching that says, Where there's lack of faith, there's lack of good faith. That's a heavy teaching. A lot of folks kick and scream when they hear that one. They don't like to hear it. But if you want to be like folks who do heavy things, that's the level that they're working at. You have to be sure you're not pretending to don't be confident so that nobody will think you're on a trip. Some people go around pretending that they don't know where it's at so that nobody will think they're on a trip, when they do sometimes really know where it's at. But they don't really know where it's at because they pretend not to. If you're doing a good thing, swing on; get heavy. There are times when I don't know what to do next, and I say, "Well, I've come to the end of a thing here, and I've got to look around and find out what to do next." There are other times when there's a series of Farm crises come on me and I think, "I know exactly what to do next." When there's nothing happening I might not know what to do next, but when it's heavy I always know what to do next. You really do too, if you've got the nerve to just up and do what you know you have to do when it's heavy. People do it all the time. The tabloids have a story every now and then of some lady who tears the doors off a wrecked semi and drags the truck driver out.

(Question.) He says he met some people who hassled him and told him that there's no hope. Well, what you do is say, "Remember me. and when you learn better, look me up."

(Question.) He said some people came through here and folks didn't like how they were touching. I don't know; I wasn't there. You're talking about a question of taste, and I don't know what the taste of that was like. I know that I can sit and watch some people smooch and it's very pretty and a gorgeous thing to watch. And I know other people that I see come on so lustful that it makes me think they're spreading germs. The thing about me touching people is that I have a personal one-to-one agreement with everybody I touch. Some folks on the Farm have let me know that they really like that, and some folks have let me know that they'd just as soon I didn't get into them too much. Once in a while I will get into somebody who doesn't seem to want it, if I see they have some uptightness or something that I can do a little spot healing on. Sometimes I pick somebody up and crack their back, shake them.

Energy can be transmitted between people. That's the reason we are the way we are about it; people have the right to their energy and how they want to be with it. I don't think we do such an austere yoga, but some people think we do. It's for the purpose of trying to be as stoned as possible all the time, and to have the kind of stoned that we can transmit to our children—a strong community and family stoned, which is what makes any tribe strong.

Some folks who come through don't practice their yoga. I'm not down on them if they don't practice their yoga, but if they want any great amount of energy from me, they've got to plug up their other end enough that it won't just be dissipated. I might want them to do a few yogas before I lay much juice on them, just so they can learn to contain it. Another thing about healing is that you have to put some energy on somebody and then teach them how to maintain it, because you aren't going to be able to sit around and give them some all the time. They ought to learn how to maintain their own.

We have a very highly developed tantric tradition on the Farm. Part of the evidence of that is our midwives. All the doctors think our statistics are fantastic, and a lot of what we do different than doctors do is we touch people with our hands instead of chrome instruments, which seems to get them off better. So this whole touch thing is not something random. Some of the single folks would like to become family folks, and part of our tantric folklore is that you have a better chance of really having a good marriage if you have a good head of steam on and a lot of juice on when you go into it. It'll naturally help you be with who your right person is, because a couple of folks who have a lot of juice on will just spark together and do it. So some folks are saving the cake, and they don't want anybody sticking their finger through the icing. When we go out on the road, I get about an equal amount of trouble from people about our birth rate on one hand, and how puritanical we are on the other.

Some teachers try to make it look as though there are a lot of different meditation techniques because they want to establish a market for a particular brand name. But the human brain is the human brain, and God is God, and the Universe is the Universe, and you pretty much have to come right down the Santa Fe there, or you just aren't going to have any action.

I think the progression they go through in Zen meditation is about as clean as any. You start off, to keep your mind from wandering, by counting your breaths, one to ten, and then ten, nine, eight, back down to one. You do that for a while, and the first thing you'll notice is that you'll space out and forget you're counting and remember minutes later that you were counting, or you'll find yourself going *fourteen . . . fifteen . . . sixteen . . .* But in time you'll be able to do that. It shouldn't be too easy or too hard—if it's too easy then you're being superficial about it.

Then you go to just following your breath with your mind, in and out, without counting. You free your mind of the numbers and just follow your breath. Your breath is an automatic metronome for your attention system. It has to keep going or you'll fall over. So you do that until you can do that pretty clean and you have a good streak going, and then you can forget your breath. When you forget your breath, you can just go to a clean, high-minded place. That's called *shikan-taza,* and it's sort of the backbone of Zen meditation. I mostly let the thoughts in my mind bubble until I recognize them for being background noise and distraction, and then I can cut loose and cut loose until I get back to a clean observer who's just watching. Then it becomes a question of just managing your energy and your rushes. There's a way to handle a shiver or a shudder so it gets you high or so that it shakes you a little bit. All those shivers and shudders are kundalini rushes if you know how to use them right—you can just sit right down on top of a shudder and make it percolate on through your system, make it come right up through you. It really gets you stoned; there's a lot of power in that stuff. Every so often you get to surfing so fast on your energy that you forget everything, and then you notice yourself again a little later down the road. You're usually pretty clean when you come back and notice yourself and say, "Oh, here it is."

(Question.) He wants to know how to get up out of a low juice place. That's probably pretty relevant right now, because folks who went through the flu are going to have to be working themselves out like that. You just have to do a little bit every day and don't overdo, because if you overdo you'll knock yourself back more. It's like growing your muscles back again. You have to build back physically and psychically. I'm still building back from the penitentiary. Every week I remember a way that I used to be that I took for granted, and I just stumble onto it again and I say, "Oh, far out. I forgot I used to be like that." Because the penitentiary was a conditioning yoga to try to take as much of that off me as possible.

(Question.) He says folks swear. One of the heaviest things that happened to me in the penitentiary was that I had to hear God's name used like that several hundred times a day, every day. If it's somebody you're close to, you can tell them. If it's too outrageous, you just can't be around it. A lot of the folks who use that kind of language say they aren't religious. Well, let them think up something of their own to swear with, because if they aren't religious that doesn't belong to them, and they aren't supposed to use it.

(Question.) That therapist doesn't believe in vibrations, so he doesn't realize that turning anger out on people just makes you self-indulgent. When I was fourteen or fifteen I used to re-run heavy scenes in my mind—scenes where I didn't make out very well—and I would re-run them so that I came out better, or maybe just the same scene and not liking it. I had a job at the time where I stood in one place and sealed up little packages, and I'd get so into running something like that in my mind that my facial expressions would be changing with it and I'd be really into it. Standing there doing that kind of work and doing that in your head is a machine for getting yourself nutty. I have a picture of me at about fifteen or sixteen years old, and every time I look at it, it makes me shudder and shake. I'm just so grateful that I didn't continue any further down the path that *he* was on. When somebody's running something around in their mind like that, they're putting out the vibration of it on everybody, just like a wood stove throws off heat when you put wood in it. You ought to be able to put together a few little experiments to communicate to this person that there are such things as vibrations.

(Question.) Some swami says he keeps anger in his pocket and just brings it out to clear up injustices. Well, I don't think it's fair to carry brass knuckles. I think we're all supposed to go bare-handed. No, anger is never necessary, anger is always a failing. When you do it it's a failing. But, as Hazrat Inayat Khan said, certain pieces of information are best conveyed in a relatively loud tone and in a lively rhythm. Just so long as you know that that's what you're doing, and don't get carried away and get mad.

(Question.) If your kid is trying to pretend to you that he has an inside and an outside and you are on the outside and what he wants to do is on the inside, and there isn't anything you can do about it, the only thing you can do is truly understand that he has no inside and no outside, and if you speak to him he will hear you. He doesn't have any ear-lids, so just tell him things until you get a reaction.

(Question.) Compulsive behavior? Well, it isn't any big deal. It's thinking it's a big deal that makes it compulsive. You can stop doing anything. When I first quit smoking cigarettes I kept reaching in my pocket, so I quit wearing shirts with that kind of pockets, and I quit reaching in my pockets.

(Question.) He said I spoke about insanity being at my back door. Well, the way you say insanity at my back door makes it sound like the wolf is at the door. I see some people out there identifying with that. I didn't say it was at my back door, I said it's just my back yard. I have walked out there frequently, I don't need a map anymore.

(Question.) One of the teachings about kids is that you don't bribe them, and especially you don't bribe them with food, because it gives them a weird, desirous, lustful attitude about food and makes it hard for them to eat what's good for them. If kids are going to have candy, they should just at some arbitrary time or other have some, so it isn't a big deal. It's the big deal made about it that makes it into a lust object and something that they'll do a lot of behind your back. Food should be something we don't have praise/blame about; food should be something that we care that everybody has enough of. You shouldn't look at food from the point of, "Oh my, what an excruciating taste sensation this is going to be. I'm hardly going to be able to stand it." The amount of goodies you give your kid should be your choice, because you are the karmic regulator of your kid's diet. It is really difficult to walk a middle path, but the middle path is the only one that is worthwhile. It's easy to slide off into extremes, and you get into more prohibitions and more rules and more regulations than you need. I am really dedicated to us keeping the faith and the agreements on what rules we have, and not multiplying them and not creating any more than are absolutely necessary for our functioning. This country has more laws than people. Every time somebody spoke truth and fearlessly put down truth in the law book, a liar has come along and commented on it and muddied it up so it's hard to interpret. So we don't want to get into, "No, don't do this, don't do that." Just be reasonable.

(Question.) The karma of the American Indian? Well, you think that karma has something to do with deserving. That's why you think there's something strange about the karma of the American Indian. I look at the karma of the American Indians and I see that, given the circumstances, the karmic laws were fulfilled. The culture with the most guns and the least morals took the goodies.

History is said to be a record of crime: it's who took what away from who, and how many guns it took to do it. Spiritual history is a different thing, and I think that the American Indians, from all that I've been able to learn about them, were really a highly developed spiritual civilization, much more so than the people who conquered them. They were not conquered by a superior philosophy, but just by more guns. They had a superior philosophy, but they were pacifists.

Being a pacifist is a heavy trip. The people who lived in this territory where we live had a tradition where there were red stick villages and white stick villages. Red stick villages had a tradition of warriors and that kind of thing, and white stick villages would be religious villages. If it came to some kind of a big issue where the people of the village were split about whether

46

to go to war or not, they'd paint the white pole in the center of the village red, and all the folks who wanted to go to war would go and hit that pole, and that would be their vote to go to war. Then all those folks would split the village together, and they'd paint the stick white again and it would be a white stick village again. The white stick village was supposed to stay that way because it was a sanctuary.

(Question.) He wants me to speak about Hermes Thrice Majestic who I mentioned in *Monday Night Class*. I'm not really talking about old Hermes too much—he's nice, but he's been dead for so long. He was called Hermes the Thrice Majestic because he was the avatar, magician-scientist and king. Three crowns. He was also said to be active in the material plane, the astral plane, and the spiritual plane, which is also three crowns. He was supposed to be so heavy as a human, real-life person that the myth of the Greek god Hermes was drawn from him. He was supposed to be this very heavy dude who knew where it was really at. All of his laws are expressed in the fabric and the being of the Farm, which is where they really need to be.

(Question.) You have parents who are alcoholics? Mainly, don't be judgmental and just understand. Don't look for truth in alcohol. Don't fall out of love with them because they lied to you about booze, because they're going to lie to you about booze. Folks who are into scag are going to lie to you about scag, and folks who are into reds and downers are going to lie to you about that. You have to love them anyway. You can't cut loose just because they lie to you about that stuff. Just love them, and try to get them something to do; they're just bored. Alcohol structures your time like television does—it gives you something to do.

I would like folks to consider being astronauts, going out to other Farms. We have several Farms out there without too many folks on them who need a little juice to get started. You're probably going to come back and see us pretty frequently, and we'll probably come to see you frequently, and we're all going to keep doing the thing. We've got to be in cahoots clear around the planet. Good morning. God Bless you. I love you all.

April 26, 1976

High States of Consciousness

Sometimes I think I should make more strenuous efforts to talk about strictly religious subjects on Sunday morning. Then sometimes I think — *How can I avoid talking about God when everything is God, and whatever I talk about is God, and the ears that hear it is God, and the mind that tries to understand it is God, and the room we sit in is God, and what's to say?*

While we were all in New York I kept getting that thing that I get when I go out on the road: "Give me your teachings in a nutshell so I'll know where you're at." I told this one dude that if we converted massive amounts of action in the world to non-profit collective hippie-type enterprises out of the profit-making ones, we could get into the action big enough to disturb some folks. If we did that *and* were obnoxious and armed ourselves, we'd be squashed for it. But if we were really harmless, really honest and really sincerely religious and cared about other people and were not doing it just for ourselves, we might get so far down the line before anybody noticed, that it would be too late.

I think that this country right now is undergoing the same revolution that went on twenty-five hundred years ago in India. That was when there was a religious consciousness that said learn to hold your breath and learn to do all those things, learn to get yourself high, and you'll become One with everything. Well, Lord knows, I love high states of consciousness. But in the light of the number of people in the world that are hungry, and the condition of this country as it relates to other countries, sometimes I get so tired of hearing that stuff.

More and more I'm beginning to like Mahatma Gandhi. He said he wanted the millions of people in India to be happy and to be healthy in order that they may grow in Spirit. What our teaching is becomes clearer and clearer to me, in the sense that *to develop a cheap and livable and graceful lifestyle is one of the most important and heaviest things that we can pass on to mankind, as a teaching to everyone.* That includes how to get along together; how to think beautifully and accurately; how to learn to govern ourselves. Govern yourself. On a truck they have a thing called a "governor" and it means that they've determined that the engine works best at a particular speed. So no matter how hard you put your foot down on the gas, when you get up to the best possible speed for efficiency of the fuel, for not tearing the truck up, and for making it last as long as possible, it will limit you to that level. Not that you can't go as hard as you can go, but it defines what is as hard as you can go.

Economists talk about management and labor, or capital and labor, having different viewpoints, and that the union system is the system whereby these two different viewpoints can work out their differences. E.F. Schumacher, in a book on economics called *Small is Beautiful,* points out that for the materialistic society, the working out of the differences between these two viewpoints is the answer to the problem. The ideal situation for production, management, and capital is complete production, with no employees and no payroll whatsoever. The ideal of the employees would be complete income with no work at all. He says that these two viewpoints are trying to work themselves out through labor hassles and stuff. The materialistic economic viewpoint is the least amount of work that you can do for the most possible amount of money. He also says that there's a Buddhist economic viewpoint in which the functions of work are defined as a *laboratory wherein a person*

may improve himself by working out against the Universe: a field of endeavor where people can reduce their ego by working together with other people for a common cause, and produce the amount of stuff it takes for the people to make it. I keep saying I am not political and I'm really not. I'm really spiritual. I find myself out in the middle of economics from meditating about Spirit and God as hard as I can.

I know exactly what we are doing here. I know the difference between what we're doing and what we ought to be doing. I know some of you have been here long enough to know that difference, how well we are doing as measured against our ideals. How do we really do our thing when no one's looking? Do folks be all one and really friendly, until they get away from their neighbors and nobody's around, and then continue their family fight?

It comes around to how much responsibility each one of us takes for what we're doing here.

There's all kinds of esoteric religious teachings about how to clear your mind by doing a mantra. *Om mani padme Hum,* or *Lord Jesus, forgive me, a sinner.* You run them through your head to blank out your thoughts so you don't be self-conscious. It's also quite difficult to be self-conscious while handling a chain saw. It's very difficult to be self-conscious while giving your best to a child. It's difficult to be self-conscious while doing a good job at anything.

We have all these senses which it must be lawful to use, or we would not have them. That materialistic idea of the world says, "Well, you have machines doing all the production, and then you have all these people who don't have anything to do, and then you have to turn the rest of the world into a giant Disneyland so the people have something to do. It's a way to exercise their senses." That consists of shooting galleries and roller-coasters. But we already have the world here which needs all this stuff done, in which we can try ourselves out, and grow and exercise ourselves in every way.

There's a lot of folks who don't try quite as hard when I'm not around. I don't know exactly how my presence makes a difference. On some levels, some folks are praise-and-blamers. If they figure I am not around to say, "Good job," they aren't going to try hard; or if I am not around to say, "Get off your tail," then they aren't going to try hard. Folks like that are doing this for some reason other than the sake of mankind. I try to be as unreliable as possible about passing out Brownie points. I try to be just as arbitrary as I can possibly be without making folks think I don't love them.

How well we do in taking care of each other is seen by everybody who comes and looks at the Farm. They look at our general level of existence and see how well we take care of each other, which is their index about whether what we're doing here is worthwhile enough to be good for export. Is this an interesting thing? A phenomenon? Is it something a sociologist would like to study? *Or is it something that is possibly a viable life-style for hundreds of millions of people?* Being voluntary peasants is a very deep and heavy spiritual teaching. Maybe deeper and heavier than anything you accomplish in the lotus position.

The problems of the United States and the world are not going to be cured by importing a religion from a country where everyone is starving. A religion has to be *mahayana*—your brothers' keeper—on a global basis. We are global, and that is what makes us different from our preceding forefathers for the last couple of million years. It used to be that if you didn't like what was going on, you could go over the mountain to another valley and do your thing. You can't go over the mountain to another valley and do your thing anymore because there's somebody living there already. There is a critical mass of population on the planet.

Planetary consciousness is not a luxury enjoyed by an avatar for which he is worshipped. It is the necessity of all the citizens of the planet in order to have a high enough level of consciousness to don't eat each other alive.

In New York the garbage was piled on the sidewalks higher than your head for a hundred feet at a time. In some of the most expensive and fanciest stores in New York, you couldn't see the window displays or the door because the garbage was piled too high, all the way down the block in front of them. And the folks were good to each other. New York had the best vibes that we've ever seen it have, because a bedraggled-looking hippie and a rich executive would have to find themselves bumping into each other while picking their way through garbage. There was a great fellow feeling. I tried to express that when I talked to the folks in New York. But I said something at one of the gigs that scared them a little bit, and it was kind of funny. I said that one of the reasons that New York City has so much better vibes than it used to is that something very cold and chilly from Bangladesh reached out halfway around the world and touched New York City and frosted the edge of the leaves and turned them brown a little bit. And a bunch of people got up and walked out.

I said at one point, while talking about tantra and love, that real old-fashioned, sweet and innocent pure love had the most electricity in it. It was the best kind, the one with the most juice. The folks who were into black leather, and whips and stuff like that were not the sexual experts, but were the people who didn't know anything—they were trying to get off in some blinded fashion. And a bunch of people got up and walked out.

Over and over again I got the question of, "Oh, you're doing pretty good now, but what would happen if you died?" Well, I'd hate to have to test that just to find out. But the closest thing to a test of it we're going to get is that I'm going to be on the road more in the future than I have in the past. We have to get out farther, and get to more folks. And you're going to have to keep the toilet paper dry while I'm gone. You're going to have to *have* some to keep dry.

Sometimes it seems to me that I almost never get to see the folks who really make the Farm work, because they're out working so hard I never see them. Who I see a lot is the folks who are having a hard time. They say the squeaky wheel gets the grease. Well, the more that you love one another and take care of one another really good, the less necessity there is for me to have to go to exceptional circumstances: I can go around and be part of the real-life everyday running of it, which is what I ought to be into more. I don't get much chance to go to the tractor barn or the motor pool or out to the fields— to go and get where people are working. The thing that makes that hard to handle is the folks who are on their own trip and who don't help take care of other folks on the Farm. We have to survive at a little higher level. We have to get a little smarter. We have to cooperate a little better. We have to use our resources a little better. We have to be a little more selfless about getting out and getting some bread for the Foundation so the Foundation can take care of you.

I feel that you ought to be thinking about the *whole thing,* and not just thinking about yourself. You ought to be thinking about how the ways we live are a teaching, and that we can't do it half-assed, because it's going to be diluted as it goes out. The bigger it gets, the less clear the teaching is going to be. This is like making a mold out of which a million parts are going to be stamped. If this mold is a little sloppy, and we really don't keep the agreements, and say, "Well, most of the time except for a McDonald-burger," then it makes the mold a little sloppy. By the time it's stamped out a million of them you won't hardly be able to tell what it was anymore. As witness, Christ tried to make such a pure mold that He let himself be killed to show what *really* being a pacifist was about, and what non-violence was *really* about. As hard as He tried to lay that Word down, within a few hundred years there were religious wars in His name. It means you've got to *really* consider what are the ideals of what we are doing. If you don't understand them, if you just got here, or if you have been here a while and don't really understand them, then you ought to be finding some way to study them. You ought to be finding someone you can ask about it. You ought to be studying it as if your life depended on it, because it does—it's all the same.

We're like a seed. Well, we're better than a seed because we have sprouted. We're like a little seedling about three-quarters of an inch high. A little frost could nip it, or somebody could step on it accidentally. We have to grow that little seedling up until it flowers and produces more seeds. If you were on a desert island and you had one grain of wheat and the intention to feed yourself some bread, you would plant that grain of wheat, and you'd take *good* care of it, until it grew up and produced ten or fifteen grains a head, and then you'd plant those ten or fifteen grains. We're just like that—trying to grow people here who understand sufficiently well enough to go out. A lot of you folks are going to have to go out and really be strong enough to help.

I hope this doesn't sound grandiose to the point of insanity, but I really feel like a whole lot of the future of this generation depends on the quality of the relationships in every household on the Farm. The quality of our relationship is going to make the difference whether this is an interesting flash in the pan, or whether it's the beginning of something that can be a change. Can we put something together that is peaceful enough that it doesn't get squashed, and is strong enough to survive? That could make a difference for a lot of people, and give an alternative to 1984. Man, it's already 1976. We're the most viable alternative to 1984 that's happening. Bigger science, more money, bigger dams, and bigger centralization—it's not going to do it. It's going to create bigger cities, bigger slums, harder garbage pick-ups, and more race riots.

Quality of existence. That seems like a real good thing to take home and think about. You can read some Holy books; you can read some Lao Tsu or the *Bible,* or something like that. You can also read Marshall McLuhan; *Understanding Media* is a Holy book. Theodore Reich, *Listening with the Third Ear* is a Holy book. Anything that tells you about the human mind, and how people get along together, anything about some kind of world-wide economics that teaches you about the state of the world is a Holy book.

We are
our brother's keeper.

And our brother is
the population of
the planet.

On these thoughts, I will let you go. Good morning. God Bless you.

December 21, 1975

A Bright Light

When we talk about God, first we mean the all, Totality. Out to the last, last edge of the Universe—which doesn't have an edge. It just goes on and on. All of it is what we first mean when we say God. Then, as a subheading under that, there is life. All life, down to its most simple form. And then, as another subheading under that, there is intelligent life, which includes plants.

We don't think that God has an ego, or that God is self-conscious, in that sense. Now there are two ways to not be self-conscious. One is to not notice yourself. The other is to be so totally looking out that you never look back. God has an intelligence—not of the kind you and I have, which is linear and depends on our conscious memories to make judgements, but an intelligence that's larger than that: looser, not as cohesive, but infinitely more massive and larger. In the mind, it is said, we have a model of the Universe. We have the Universe out there and we have a model of the Universe in here. And we do operations with our models of the Universe, and then try them out in the real world and see if they work.

God is not separate from the Universe. God is only One. The Universe itself is God's mind; and the flow of everything is God's thoughts. And praying to us really means *to try to be an intelligent synapse in God's mind,* a synapse that is not going to trigger for violence, no matter what. Love, connect. And we affect the mind of God by being free will synapses.

Sometimes people ask me, "What can we do? What's it about?" There's a really simple answer. It's very hard to do anything about it, but the answer is simple enough. Why are people being that way to each other? Any people? Anywhere? Why is that happening? Well, it's ego, ain't it now? Ain't it just that some folks think it's okay to do it to some other folks, over anything—no matter what the cost, no matter who those folks are. That's ego.

So what can you do about it? The first thing you can do about it is to see about your own.

You may not think that's connected, or that it makes a difference. But a thing happened while we were up in New York

that was really a beautiful teaching. We were parked out by the trucking docks down by the Hudson River. It was morning, and Albert was going to talk to the Farm on the ham radio. Well, the way the antennas are wired up on the Greyhound, the whole bus is an antenna. It's long and has a big old flat side to it. Albert said, "Fire up the bus and move a little bit." So we fired it up, and started driving around the parking lot in a tight little circle. So we came around that circle, we turned around and around and around, and suddenly the radio started coming on loud—and it got

louder and louder and louder until we got to a point. And when we went past that point it started to fade again, and we backed up to that place again. We were lining the bus up with a piece of wire strung out by the barn in Tennessee—a piece of wire that was a thousand miles away. And when it was lined up, it was a lot stronger.

If you bring a loving and egoless place into your heart—if you be really loving, and really open, and really want to help out your brother—you can line yourself up with a giant antenna. And it will make your signal a lot stronger. It will make the signal itself a lot stronger, too, because then you'd be a repeater station: one of those microwave antennas out there on the hilltop that picks up the signal coming this way and amplifies it and puts it back out.

That signal from God is kind of like the sun. There's the amount of sun you can feel on your face—a certain amount of warmth. You say, "Well, here I feel this little piece of warmth. It's nice, but it's not too strong." But when you consider that you're ninety-three million miles away from it, and you're getting that much, that's really putting out a bunch, ain't it?

If you can go into your heart of hearts and get really quiet and really kind and really truthful with yourself, you can feel a little something. It's like that sunshine.

We're trying to bring something into the world. We're trying to manifest something into the world. Manifested means it's already there latently; but you want to bring it out into the world.

Let me tell you about the Baal Shem Tov, the Hassidic master from Europe. "Baal Shem Tov" means "Master of the Good Name," or "Master of God's Name." Now they say that his father was a very pious man, and that his father wanted to bring a son into the world that would be a help to all mankind. He prayed for that for seventy years or so: to bring a strong son into the world to help all mankind.

There was a soul in Heaven that was very bright—tremendous light. And that soul felt the old man's prayers, and wanted to be born, to be his son, to do that thing. The way the story goes, that soul was so strong and so powerful that he frightened Satan, and made Satan angry, with the idea he was going to get loose into the world. Satan knew that if *that one* ever got loose, . . .

So every time the old man would pray for that son, all the angels would agree and say, "Hey, he's such a good man and he has such a good thing he wants to do."

And then Satan would come up and plead the other cause. He'd say, "Maybe he just wants that son so he can say, 'My son the Savior.' Maybe he just wants that son to show what a heavy father he is. Maybe he just wants that son for himself for some reason."

And the angels said, "No, listen to his prayers, what a good man."

And Satan would propose tests. The Baal Shem Tov's father was offered a very beautiful princess and the throne of the kingdom. And he said, "No, I just want to have my son. I want to have this son that's going to come be the Savior. I don't want to be heir of the kingdom. I don't want to marry this beautiful princess."

And the angels said, "See? See?"

And Baal Shem Tov's father had to undergo many tests, similar to the kinds of tests Jesus had to undergo, being tempted—to see if he was *really* doing it for everybody. Well, the Baal Shem's father was so pure that he passed all the tests, and he had a son.

When he was born, his parents were both a hundred years old. And Satan, in cahoots with the angel of death as usual, said, "Well, he may get born, but his mother's had *her* time and I'm going to take her now."

And the angels all got together and everyone prayed, and they said, "You know, if he's going to come do it for everybody, he ought to have a mother."

And one of the other people in Heaven said, "Look here, I was supposed to have twenty years more, but the angel of death came and got me. The system owes me twenty years, and I want to give that twenty years to the Baal Shem Tov's mother so he can have a mother." And they had to go for it, because all the tzaddiks agreed. The tzaddiks are all the just men; and the just men are so just that if they all agree on something, then God has got to do it. That's *just!* So the just men all agreed that it had to happen.

And so he got in, and was a heavy teacher.

We're trying to manifest something heavy into the world. We're trying to bring a bright soul down into the world, where people can understand it. And if we don't do right, nobody will believe us. If they say, "You're doing it for yourself," nobody will believe us. We have to *really* remember that what we're doing here is not just for us. But it's really for everybody.

It means we can't be on our own trip at the expense of the whole thing. That's not something we just do on Sunday. I'm not saying that it's not a meditative place; but that's something that's with us all through the week, in every phase and every part of our lives, in every little thing we do. That's where that difference is made. *I really know we're all One. And I really know if we're trying to do a good thing that we'll get a lot of help. We're standing in a really nice position to be a lot of help to a lot of people. And that gives me so much strength and so much contentment that, even with the condition the world is in, there's a certain amount of contentment. Not that it's all covered. Not that it's cool.* **But that there's something you can do; and that it's within your power to do it, and it makes a difference if you do it.**

In order to do this heavy thing, I request that a bunch of you people heavy up. I want a bunch of you people to heavy up and start carrying some mail yourselves. It's fun, it's good karma, travel and adventure . . .

It's not that we have particularly accomplished anything. It's that we're in a position that we might be able to try to accomplish something. And if you think we've had to hustle so far, you ain't seen nothing yet.

March 30, 1975

McLuhan talks about the medium as the message—that it isn't just what's on the television set; it's the fact that the information is being transmitted at all, no matter what it is: the medium is the message. We're trying to derive a discipline that is an exact and real discipline of how to move and how to do it, that embodies in every way the principles we try to live by—not just as a set of motions you perform with numbers on each motion on the stage, but every way you move. Everything you be. Every way you do it with somebody. Every way you deal with yourself. What we are trying to evolve here is a free and open pattern of sanity—but nonetheless a pattern—in order that people may be sane in a cultural context that supports them for being sane, rather than supporting them for *not* being sane, as a matter of cultural knowledge that every little kid and everybody in the community should share as they grow up. Now it used to be that way. Lao Tsu said the governments were invented when people forgot how to *be* on the natch.

The Farm has grown, and lots of people have come. There are unspoken assumptions that have been diluted; they haven't been passed on much because they weren't spoken, so some of those unspoken assumptions that most of the folks on the Farm know, we've begun to violate a little bit. We're too young to afford any cultural drifts. If we got a whole lot of cultural drift at this age, we won't be recognizable in twenty years. I ask you to be conscious, at that level, of what goes on around you.

For example, there are folks who come to the meditation talking about what they're going to do at work tomorrow, or what happened last night, as they come right down into the meditation talking—as if, because all these people are being quiet, they are somehow not able to hear; when in fact, it is one giant with about eight hundred ears. And it not only hears the people walking up and back, but it hears when a car parks back up the road, and can tell whether the car has power steering by the sound the front wheels make on the gravel when they turn. And a dog chasing a deer out through that canyon over there, and there's a shot of somebody deer hunting way back over there on the other side. It is a really intelligent, sensitive instrument gathered together and quiet enough for it to be all one thing. *It is tremendously powerful, tremendously sensitive, and to be treated with great respect.* **It is the people.** *Sangsara and Nirvana are one; and so are the people and God.*

When we look back to the Magna Carta we say that it charts some of the basic freedoms under which we live, and that it's one of the earliest documents about freedom of any kind. But when the document was done, it was not for the people at all; it was for the barons. It established the relationship of the barons to the crown; it did not guarantee anything about the people. There were serfs whose life was not their own, whose rights were not guaranteed under the Magna Carta at that time. However, you have to notice down the line here, the difference between being busted in the United States and being busted in Mexico. The difference is that the United States follows old English common law as the basis of the Constitution on down to now; it says the burden of proof is on the state, and you are presumed innocent until proven guilty. The Code of Napoleon, which most European laws are derived from, has no such provision. It says you have to prove you're innocent. And that basic assumption makes the difference in how you're treated.

There's no one who is expendable. That's one of our key assumptions. There are some others. Back in San Francisco, I used to say that I was the one-man-one-vote guru: there isn't really supposed to be an intermediary between you and God; although some religions teach the necessity of an intermediary. Some religions think of Jesus as a gateman to Heaven—who you have to get straight with before you can go in—instead of being *the spiritual vibration itself, which if you are in contact with, you automatically become in contact with Heaven—and if you're in good enough shape to touch it, it will touch you back.*

(Q.: Where does ambition fit in here?) Ambition is a personal drive. A person driven by ambition will just walk on everybody on the way. If you are going to be driven, be driven by something that's for everybody. Ambition causes you to have tropisms toward evil things. I'll give you an example of that. Somebody who's ambitious may not realize the principle that you can't climb very high in an unafraid society. If the society is not afraid, one man can't climb very far above the rest of the people—not in a sense of attainment, but in a sense of power and ambition. But if he scares the people, the people become a more rigid structure, and he can climb higher and farther: so he will tend to condition towards a rigid structure in order to keep his ladder solid. That's how Hitler got in: he just conditioned the whole society into a pyramid that he could climb, be on top of, and do his number from. It was a terrified society.

And Chief Davis is still powerful in Los Angeles. He got his juice from the Watts riots. The Watts riots convinced the people of L.A. that there was a dangerous rabble there; and Davis just rides that all the time. He talks about, If you don't keep giving me more men, and more guns, and more nightsticks, and a bigger paramilitary SWAT team, the dangerous rabble's going to get you. He keeps that whole area a little scared.

Now, Patricia Hearst was the daughter of a mighty prince. That was all she knew; and then she began to bug out on him. She had a boyfriend with long hair, and she was smoking a little grass over in Berkeley already—which *she* thought was revolutionary. The people that kidnapped her didn't think so. She was Patricia Hearst and it didn't matter whether she turned on or not. So, they took her head for a while, and she said what they wanted her to say. She used to say what her daddy wanted her to say, then she said what they wanted her to say. Then the government got her and she said what they wanted her to say for a while; and then F. Lee Bailey, Attorney, got her and she said what he wanted her to say for a while. There isn't any Patricia Hearst. There's just this puppet that several people have been talking through, over a period of years. She has hardly any free will at all, she's so conditioned and neurotic. I feel very sorry for her, like a lost soul.

(Q.: How about the amount of publicity that thing got?) That publicity was for Chief Davis who shot down the S.L.A. The reason he could do that was because of previous violence which had given him the permission and the special emergency powers to have that well-armed attack squad of police. They dealt with the S.L.A. as a purely military operation, and burned them out like a bunker in a battlefield. That's probably the worst thing that was every shown on television—just really an evil thing, because it breached the compassion so badly. It made many people afraid and many people paranoid and sowed terror and violence in the hearts of all kinds of people, not just Hearsts and Fords and people like that who are afraid of having their kids kidnapped, but all the poor hippies, and all the poor black people in Los Angeles who have to live under Chief Davis, who gets to be a tyrant because the people are afraid.

California acts like two states, and Jerry Brown is the prince of Northern California. In Southern California he's like Richard the Lion-Hearted having to work it out with King John and the Sheriff of Nottingham. Davis has so much juice and the movie industry and Orange County are so reactionary; and San Diego has whole neighborhoods where retired Navy commanders live. San Diego is a military town. Lockheed and the Marines and Navy and big aircraft and shipyards—that makes a military town.

(Q.: How do you get barons and how do you keep them from happening?) Ambrose Bierce's definition of piracy is: Commerce just as God made it, without all the fol-de-rols. Bucky points out that at one time the Vikings took over whole areas of coast because they had communication. They could come in and strike and get back in their boats and split, and nobody could follow them. They had a superior communication, so they became the pirates. Henry Morgan was a pirate, just like Black Beard. He became the governor of Jamaica because he had the most gunboats in the Caribbean. Well that's not new; Pancho Villa was given one of the states of Mexico. They said, "Look, we aren't going to give you the whole country. Settle for a state and we'll leave you alone!" That's how barons come out—they come out by force. John D. Rockefeller either bought or destroyed all his competition. He said he felt that he was acting directly under orders from his creator to make as much money as he possibly could, which he was then going to distribute to worthy people. One of the reasons that I have Will Rogers as one of the saints in my pantheon is that when Will met John D. Rockefeller, he gave *Rocky* a dime.

What keeps the barons from taking over is that people take the responsibility on themselves to safe-guard the freedoms of the people.

July 5, 1976

Right Livelihood

I always say you're supposed to keep a good meditative consciousness on all the time. But I never really realize how far short I fall of that until I sit down and meditate for a while and get it on, and discover what a difference there was from when I got here to now. I came here this morning from a fast couple of weeks, with a lot of things on my mind. I sat down, and the first thing that happened was that you all had been meditating for about twenty minutes by the time I got here. I sat down— and all that noise in my mind was immediately amplified. So I had to sit there and deal with these things, and think them over. So I kept thinking that there's a consciousness. *Don't forget about the consciousness, because there's stuff that won't even look the same, if you really raise your level of consciousness.* And stuff fell in proportion. And it got to where I could see what was important and what wasn't important, and what I should be doing.

One of the things I was thinking about when I was meditating this morning was the question of right livelihood. It's just a fine question to think about on a Sunday morning. It's really important: how we relate to the other folks in the world, the other folks in poor countries, the other folks in rich countries, other folks like us all around the world, of whom there's a gang.

It is said that Buddha got up and did his morning meditations, and walked into town with his begging bowl, going around from house to house knocking on doors until they gave him food. Then he ate that, and he went back and didn't eat the rest of the day. As thinly populated as the world was in those days, and with no media as we now know them—his word was not even spread by so much as a newspaper, but just by word of mouth, person to person—the amount of respect that was accorded him was incredible. I guess you'd call that *shakti* that he had, an incredible amount of *shakti*—so much that he felt it was necessary that he beg for his food. And he wasn't teaching by that to create a class of people who begged for their food—that was not his intention. He thought inasmuch as he had such awesome power, it would be a good thing if he would just keep himself grounded, and go in every day and beg for his food, to keep him connected to the real world.

But we're in another world now. And the question of how many people can the world handle has actually come up; and there are estimates, even. Fifty years' worth of this, a hundred years' worth of that. Most of what we're talking about, like coal and oil and aluminum and so forth, is expected to run out in another hundred and fifty, hundred and thirty years or so at the present projected curves. Well, it is obvious that the present projected curves are unreal, because we aren't going to run out in a hundred years. Things are going to change before we get there; but those curves are *really* going to change.

And that makes it so the question of right livelihood is more than a personal question. It becomes a question of *what is our responsibility to our fellow man?*

So we have elected as our path that we're going to take care of ourselves. The first thing we got into was farming, because we thought farming was guaranteed good karma. It *must* be okay to farm. Then we thought, "What other kinds of things can we do that are also right vocation and for mankind?" Well, if it's good to grow food, it must be good to truck it, to distribute it and get it out to the people. So those are related good karma industries. And that question becomes heavier and heavier.

Now the larger question is that *We need to have a massive religious revival and enlightenment across the country.* The country's spiritual technology has fallen into disuse and rust, from so many years of neglect, to the point where we're so ignorant about Spirit and God and love and free will, that some people are just pretty much suckers for anything that comes by, because they want something so badly. It's not just that we want something. It's that we need it.

We are just as radical as we can be—back to the root. We are trying to preserve thousands-year-old knowledge. It's not the chant you chant; it's not the name that you name God: it's how you live. And this is a school about how to live.

(Question.) He wants to talk about loving yourself. Well, the best way to love yourself is to *love all things in the Universe, not forsaking yourself.* You have to love yourself for things like being a clean machine—for carrying the incredibly complexly-coded genetic information for generations and generations and generations. That's the beauty of the actual thing. Self-regulating, self-temperature-control, all that. Very fancy! Up to and including free will and moral structure. It's very heavy equipment.

And you have to realize that harming yourself is the same as harming someone else. Because we're all One. And being bad to yourself is just as bad as being bad to somebody else. Because it puts that into the world. As far as your personality goes, if you don't pay any attention to it, maybe it will go away by itself.

We have reasons for most of the stuff we're doing: we've made most of the mistakes known to mankind so far, and we may make the rest of them before we get done. We hope to make them in such a pattern that it doesn't waste us.

Good morning. God Bless you.

June 27, 1976

A Pearl of Great Price

Consciousness is the pearl that I sold everything else to get. It says in the *Bible*, "A pearl of great price," which, if you discover it, you would be wise to sell everything that you have and buy that pearl. And for me that was consciousness, and the discovery that I could actually, consciously, relate to and understand the Universe in my waking consciousness. Some people talk about bliss and think it means all day long with your tongue hanging out the side of your mouth going ha-ha-ha. But there's a line I've heard some old Christians say which was really good: *The sober consciousness of waking bliss.* You're sitting right there, you're perfectly sane, you're perfectly awake, you're perfectly together, you know where it's at anyway, and it's cool.

The thing about consciousness is that the folks who know the least about consciousness are the ones who are the most affected by changes of it. Some folks don't know anything about consciousness at all, and it never occurs to them to think, "What's this level of consciousness like; is this a good level of consciousness? Is there a higher one I could be in? Could I get out of this level and change it?" There are people who never think things like that, who never, ever think, "Could I be in a better place than this? Is this the best place I could be, considering what's happening?" Some of those people you find in places like the penitentiary. That's how come they get there. They go through changes ranging from "Wow, I had a good time last night, Wow, I really got off," to "Muther, don't come and touch me again, I'm gonna get you," running from one level to another and never being aware that *they are moving in a medium, and that they have a choice of whether to be in those places or not.*

I remember completely, clearly, the exact instant where I first got a hold on the idea that *There's me, and there's consciousness, and I can relate to it as I choose.* I remember the instant that I had that realization; it was one of the heaviest things that ever happened to me. I take what I learned in that position and use it again and again and again, just like a good hammer in my tool kit, something that I have to take out and use a lot of times because it's useful and strong and a good tool.

I was sitting tripping with a bunch of friends and I found myself sitting in this place with my head hanging down in my lap and sort of gently parachuting downwardly, just drifting down; and getting not-very-good; and while I was drifting I remembered a teaching that I'd picked up. And it said that *your mood while you're tripping can be controlled by you if you want to, and you don't have to be in this place if you don't want to.* I made a U-turn and started coming up, and I came up and I said, "It works." And when I knew it worked it started really lifting; I mean really picking up and taking off. And I ain't never forgot it.

Sometimes I find myself sloshing around in levels of consciousness that are not real exalted. But I always know that I don't have to do that, even if it may take me a little while to figure a way out of it. Maybe I might be in a place where I can't just up and change. Maybe I have a whole bunch of karma that I have to move first. But I can know that I can change, and it can change, and I can change it and improve it and make it better.

A blessing is what comes out of your heart, not your mouth; and if your heart's pure and untroubled, then your blessings are pure and untroubled. If your heart's pure and strong, crying babies will stop crying for you, skittery horses will hold still and let you catch them. And if you didn't know anything about consciousness you'd have no control over those blessings that come from your heart. If you don't know about consciousness, you can walk around with anger in your heart, which is like walking around with a colored filter on you; so everything that comes out of you is a little anger-flavored, if you walk around with anger in your heart. It doesn't matter if you don't really express it or jump up or cuss people out and hit people. If you just have it in your

heart and walk around mad, you get mad about something.

A lot of us have been studying consciousness and have been through levels of consciousness ranging from pure disembodied intellect floating in a sea of white light and ecstasy, to just fifteen or twenty years of not knowing where you were at at all, hitting your head against a brick wall. Now when folks come on the Farm, one of the things we want to communicate, without coming on like we're hot stuff or anything, is that a lot of us have studied a discipline of consciousness for a long time. And if we see somebody who loses their temper periodically, we think they are a little loose. I know that isn't the usual opinion in the rest of the world. They say, "Everybody loses their temper now and then." We don't think that you ought to. There are people here that I haven't seen show any anger in five or six years.

In general, we think that we are as psychically healthy as we are physically healthy, pretty much across the board. That's from a lot of reasons, and they are all miraculous.

That there is a cooperation among the people to maintain a high level of consciousness is miraculous. Really. Try and look around and find this many folks dedicated to doing that. And that what we know about the mind makes us know to not be afraid. We don't panic out, or be afraid if someone looks a little loose or nutty. Most of us have been there several times. How many folks here have known that they have been nutty once? (Laughter.) See? At least that many. But there is another thing, that *this many people trying hard creates a vibration that happens psychically*—you don't learn about it with words in your head or anything, and it doesn't happen because somebody knows the same common assumptions. There isn't any signal system necessary for it to transmit. You don't have to speak language, or speak at all, or hear at all, or see at all. You can come and not be able to see, not be able to hear and not be able to speak, and you can be improved by the vibration that is here. And that vibration is a very miraculous one, because it doesn't depend on being told—you don't have to know it's happening for it to do it to you. It's objective and real. And it does it to you because it is objective and real. That's good to know. There are many millions of people in the world who don't know that. And just to know that simple, everyday thing I can say out loud and in language just like I was saying, "I live on First Road," is miraculous. Just out-front miraculous.

I wonder if anybody noticed in the meditation—we quit meditating on a high place, but back about five minutes before that it went (sound of something descending) and it just got down into kids, dogs barking and noise from other places. Did anybody notice that? Just a little bit, and then just before we started to OM, it picked up and smoothed out real nice and we quit there while we were ahead. You know, that's miraculous too—that we share those changes. It's very far out that we share those changes.

So with that kind of thing in mind, I've been thinking of us as a spiritual academy. I've been trying to figure out ways to phrase that strongly enough that it doesn't get submerged in the Farm. The Farm is a groove, but without *that* it just wouldn't last. We just wouldn't make it through the heavy trips. We'd get mad at each other and fall out of love and drift apart and go back to college, or go back to living off our mothers. Well, that's a level of discourse that I want to follow out a little bit. I feel lucky to have a nice cool day to do it with. But from this kind of good place I want to take questions of a spiritual nature—the other questions we hit our heads against all week long.

(Question.) Righteous indignation is sort of like plutonium—there's a certain amount of value in it, but it has disastrous side effects to it. And if you aren't a really fancy technician, you can't handle it without getting burnt. Righteous indignation is seductive. It feels so powerful; it feels like if you can go to bat for a good cause, you can really pull out the stops. *Be Careful.* How righteous is it? It's really dangerous.

There are effects that happen which people try to explain in different ways. One is a hypothesis where they use what they call spirits—evil spirits and good spirits, and they say that if you get stoned you can get in contact with them and stuff. It's like in the cowboy movie when an Indian comes up the canyon and says, "Don't like it. Bad. Evil spirits." Well, you could run the same movie with a hippie coming up the canyon and saying, "Hey man, bad vibes here."

This is a geography of the psychic world. In the psychic world there are forces or energy bundles or energized areas or fields that have flavors, and if you resonate with them you attract them. You can pluck one guitar string that is tuned to a good E, and another guitar tuned to an E will resonate with that string—they call them elementals. People who talk about magic also use the word "elementals." Elementals are just little clouds of emotion which, if you get them on you, you are that way. It's like if you resonate anger long enough, you can get an angry elemental on you. And then it is fed by your anger. It has no consciousness; it has no mind; it is not a living entity, but it is a force. That's why we call them elementals. It seems to be as basic as an element or something, and you can do a lot of stuff with them. But you are feeding them on your life force. They're like a bundle of tropisms. A tropism is when a flower turns toward the sun. The flower doesn't have a mind, but it turns toward the sun. The reason is that the surface of the skin of the stalk is sensitive to light, and light on the stem causes it to grow slower on the side with the light so it bends toward the light. So you can see how an effect happens with no mind outside of God's mind to make it happen.

In the same way, I saw someone attract an elemental that I referred to as an angry deity when I saw it on him. There had been a hassle going on the first several hours, and he attracted something that you attract from hassling at high revs for a while. And this dude suddenly turned into this huge thing. (You know, when you talk about the things you see, you have to remember that you aren't really *seeing* that, but you are seeing something that translates in your consciousness in terms that you can understand. So what I saw was a translation my mind made of the vibrations that was coming off this dude.) It was like a big steel breastplate of a Roman warrior with a big helmet on him and a lot of jaggedy Marvel Comic power lines coming off of him. And it said, "Power? *Power?* POWER? I don't see power, I just see people." And it was like an angry deity. They call it a deity—not God, the totality, but a being or energy that moves on other planes than ones we are used to sometimes—devas and stuff like that. That stuff is real, and it's out there, but it's not conscious. You are conscious. That stuff isn't. You dig? So when you run into that kind of stuff, you don't fight it like you're fighting somebody who is after you. You fight it like you fight a flash flood or a fire. Do you understand that? It is not like somebody's trying to get you, it's like you're in quicksand.

You can do stuff in quicksand that's the right thing to do, that will get you out of it. And when you find yourself in head places, when it does run into those kinds of vibes, it's a little bit like car racing. Take two cars racing nose-to-tail down a winding road. The one in back can pull up behind the one in front and just touch its bumper about halfway down a turn and it'll spin out. Well, if you're running anger, or you're running heavy desire-flavored emotions, you can be running along just charging that stuff powered by your own ego, and you can hook up with any elemental forces going in the same direction you're going, which can nudge you a little bit, and spin you right out. Anybody understand that?

Inasmuch as there's stuff in the Universe that will reinforce one or another aspect of you, then you have an obligation to see what you can do to attract the kind of stuff that will reinforce you in a sane, kind and loving direction. And if you're already

moving in a good sane direction and you run through an anger elemental or something like that, you just blow through it, you're already underway. Now that's a level of magic I just hardly ever talk about. But the thing about it is, it affects us whether we talk about it or not.

(Q.: How do you stay connected with good ones?) Well, by being good yourself. But that is a value judgment. Now, those things don't have any value to them. They just have effects— sleet, hail, snow, warm rain. They're different, but they aren't bad or good except as a result of a human taking them seriously and living them and giving them entrance into the real world, when they wouldn't have any entrance into the real world if somebody didn't believe in them and bring them on.

(Question.) Okay, so you're somebody who's spun out; you're a little loose. Well, that's a real good place to know about. Because at that place it's purely a free will decision to get it together or let go and say, "Well, I could use a vacation, I'll just let go and be a little nutty for a while." Instead, you have to work on principle, so that, as the various negative emotions hit you—when you're scared or you're losing it or you're getting out of control—you have to look at it, and to face it, taste it; if you run from experiencing it, it'll scare you, and it'll keep scaring you. You have to stop and face it, and when you do, naturally you're stronger in a way, you're more real. There a yogi named Mouni-Sadhu who writes books with titles like *Samadhi* and stuff. He said that if an astral projecting magician and a magician in his body met, the one in his body has more power. That means you ordinary citizens are stronger than spooks. Wouldn't it be nice if everybody knew it? But as a matter of electrical energy and power, a full-fledged living human being entity with all his stuff on has more juice than anything floating around disembodied. You're grounded, so you have the juice. If you always know that, it'll give you a little strength to make those good decisions at those times. I hesitate to talk this way sometimes for fear people will think I'm nuts, but it works for me.

(Question.) That's like when you drive a car on ice and start losing it, what you do when you start losing it makes a difference whether you make it or spin right on out. Most people who have never driven on ice have a tendency to turn the wrong way, and you have to learn to turn the other way, because your tendency, your instincts are to turn the wrong way, which will make you spin out worse, and you have to teach yourself to turn the way that doesn't spin you out. And you don't know when you're going to break loose. You don't know when you're going to run into some ice, so you have to develop a reflex that turns you the correct way right away. You can teach yourself just like you teach yourself to play the guitar or something—you have to *teach* yourself.

Since you asked that question, I want to explain what you were doing to everybody a little bit. He'd get mad and come up on folks fast, and he wouldn't know he was going to get mad until he hollered at somebody or had already blown it—and then he thinks he's all out of shape, and starts getting a little speedy and hustling, trying to catch up by working hard enough to balance his karma. All of that is from thinking that you have to *do* something, you see? The stuff you get mad about is stuff you want to do, or can't get done, or want to get done faster; and you just have to stop and say, "What'll happen if it doesn't happen? And so what?" Peace, just like after being busted.

(Q.: How does it affect you in other ways?) Well, if you meditate and be really pure, then pure resonances will stick on you— if you have pure thoughts and don't have a lot of anger and hatreds and heavy desires, if you don't have a lot of heavy disappointments. Otherwise, all that kind of stuff troubles you, and makes you tend to be an antenna and a repeater for troubled stuff.

(Q.: Are there elementals that affect us if we like them?) Yes, there are, and in fact, they are more dangerous than the anger kind. The incubus and succubus, for example, are the names of a pair of elementals, male and female respectively, which are masturbatory elementals that hang out on you when you self-indulge; they feel good, but they don't have very high vibes at all. They have quite low vibes. And they get downer as they go, but they feel good in your bod, and there are people in particular forms of what mental hospitals call nuttiness, who just lay around in ecstasy all the time, and hump and wiggle and go on and on and on like that—they've given up a certain section of their thing to running that. But that is a medieval way of thinking about something, to call it a succubus or incubus or something, and that has a value judgment, just in thinking about it that way. And that's what we are trying to bust loose from. It's not so much an incubus which an artist can draw as a demon hovering over your bed, but it's resonating resonances, all of the scales of the music of the Universe. All of the resonances are going to happen—if you have a complete orchestra all of the resonances happen—but you can make them happen at the most appropriate times and places.

(Q.: Could you talk about good vibes with food?) If you don't put a certain amount of value into your food, it isn't even nourishing. The Hindus say that the most important thing the cook puts in the food is *shakti,* which is what they call energy and life force. And they say that that's the most important factor in making the food nutritious. So when you eat the food, you have to respect the *shakti;* you have to know it's good because somebody put themselves into it, and made it be that way: it didn't just happen, and they are actually giving you some of their life force. Cooking for someone is almost like nursing them directly, there's so much of your own vibes that go into it. You have to believe that it'll average out over a period of time, and you'll get your share: you don't have to demand what you think is your share each plateful. Over a long period of time, you'll get your share. So you can relax, and don't worry about that.

I didn't know I was like that until I got to a level of consciousness one time in San Francisco when the food started coming to the table, and I was impatient and wanted people to be efficient and get the food down on the table, so we can get at it, and let me just get a bite and start eating and then you can mess around and take care of whoever you want to serve. You have to respect the *shakti* that is in the food, and to know that you aren't respectful of that if you're greedy.

(Q.: What did Jesus mean about throwing pearls before swine?) "Cast not your pearls before swine, nor give your precious things to the dogs, lest they turn and rend you." And what He meant by that was that you can't come on to people too fast. It's an unfortunate quotation, I've always thought, because there's a way it can be taken which sounds like the people are swine. And that is not what it's about. But some of the things I've said this morning, if I went into Nashville and gave pretty much the same rap I gave this morning, I'd be commitable. In the Minnesota Multiphasic Personality Inventory, a belief in God and having seen hallucinations are considered to be classic symptoms of schizophrenia. And if you went and told people a lot of metaphysical stuff that they didn't understand, without very carefully preparing them and really giving them a groundwork so that you wouldn't insult their intelligence or make them have to believe something they have no groundwork for believing in, . . .

What would a pig know to do with a pearl? The pearl would be un-understandable. That's all it really means.

And the thing about ". . . and your precious things to the dogs lest they turn and rend you,"—man, a lot of self-taught prophets have a very short life span. They go out and lay a bunch of heavy stuff on people until they burn them out and make them mad and scare them and make them weird, and then somebody comes and does them up. It's important. It's not just your own tail that you're supposed to be thinking about saving when you're doing that. It's that you're trying to not make a bad scene happen around the teachings. You don't want to have a bad scene happen around the teachings. You don't want the teachings to have a bad vibe that'll ever turn anyone away, because the teachings are so rare. I always like the way they come on about spiritual teachings in the Tibetan books: they say it's perfect in its root and perfect in its branch and perfect in its flower.

(Question.) Well, the thing she's talking about is not too rare. I know people who have taken eternal vows into half a dozen orders in the last few years. They join some order because they like the clothes or something, and then get in there and wish they weren't—and then they say, "Well, what's this like?" because leaving an order that you took a vow into is a little like getting a divorce—you don't want to do it too many times. I think part of the thing that gets you that way is in yourself and part of it is in the system of teachings that's available in the country today. And the part that's in yourself is the superstitious belief in magic wands or philosophers' stones or golden wazoos—superstitious beliefs that make you be something of a sucker, looking for stuff like that.

The other part of it is that there is a bunch of teachers around who say things like, There's a tiny blue seed, and if you don't see the tiny blue seed you don't know where it's at; or There's a little sound that goes through your head, and if you don't hear the little sound go through your head, you don't know where it's at. And these are spiritual teachers who are trying to distinguish themselves from other spiritual teachers by having a recognizable brand of lick—they pick out one or another aspect of the teachings and magnify it out of proportion as *their* thing. You have to not be superstitious about that—and you can find God, know God, be enlightened, have a heavy spiritual life and be canonized without ever having seen a little blue seed, or a little sound in your head, either—I promise you that.

Canonized is the process of being sainted; at one time the Catholic Church was getting saints so thick and so fast that they put up high standards so folks wouldn't be faking sainthood. They said a saint had to be dead for fifty years, and there had to be witnesses to the act they did. In another eighty years or so, they're going to call Mother Teresa a saint. I'm not waiting. She's a saint today. She was a saint before I ever heard of her, and I was blown. How far out to find a saint running around the earth! You don't have to wait eighty years to be canonized.

But people are caught between their desire to find the golden thingy on the one hand, and people offering the golden thingy on the other. But there is a level of consciousness that will carry you through just about everything. I would have said everything, but Jesus said at one point, "Father, why hast thou forsaken me?" Dropped his hole card just for a second. He got it back. He didn't forget it for long. But when He said that, He'd forgotten His hole card for a second, maybe under the stress and pain—but there is a level of consciousness that will carry you through.

(Question.) I'm unwilling to make too much of a dichotomy between lower selves and higher selves. I think everybody's higher self is always trying to do its best. So just don't be superstitious. There's a bunch of superstitions like that, that people are heir to. I call one of them the Western Grand Chess Master superstition, which says there's this dude off in Russia somewhere who isn't even human, that the way he plays chess is off the human scale. And it isn't true. He's human, whoever he is.

By the way, I found a nice piece of information the other day, that in the continuing chess game between mankind and the computers, so far John Henry's beating the computers. So far man is winning; there aren't any computers that consistently beat man. They have to be very sophisticated computers to even play chess at all. The way computers work is that you make a decision and there's a branch, and you make a few more decisions, and each of those makes a branch. That thing obviously doubles and redoubles pretty fast as you go down the chain. They say that if you can make a computer that can see down fifteen layers of fact, it would be the smartest entity in the world. The Russians say that whichever country develops a chess computer that can figure fifteen layers of decision, will take over the world. Now, people-type chess players hold whole banks of alternatives. They not only are playing chess, but remember going out with their girlfriend last night.

(Q.: How many layers are they in so far?) The best computer that they have so far has a basic model that does the immediate board and makes hundreds of decisions a minute, and then they have a big back-up computer that handles the heavier variables, and it can make forty thousand decisions a minute, sampling stuff, throwing stuff away that doesn't work, and resampling. But a computer is not smart. A computer counts on its fingers real fast. It can't raise its consciousness; it doesn't have any consciousness.

(Question.) About ladies as elemental forces, yes. There's some research going on about that at this time. They've noticed that if you have a bunch of ladies living together like at a college dorm or sorority house or somewhere like that, that if they stay together long enough, they will tend to start having their periods all in the same day—they'll start catching a rhythm, and will come around to all starting their periods on the same day. Then there's another area of research going on about light— that ladies respond to light, and that it changes their cycle according to the kind of light they sleep in and how dark the room is they sleep in. And the hypothesis that these scientists are following is that sleeping in the open under the moon would tend to hook you to the moon, and that man lost his connection with that rhythm by moving indoors. And the average cycle is the same as the lunar month, so the same force that makes the tides happen, making the Pacific Ocean lower and rise ten feet—heavy stuff going on—also affects ladies.

And there is stuff in your own endocrine system that will put you out like LSD; and other stuff that will be released at certain points in your birthing experiences; and other stuff that can change its flow and make you grow a beard and get a bass voice all of a sudden, or that can make you grow taller. It's interesting that in the *Bible* it says, "Swear not by God or by earth which is God's footstool, for who among you can add one cubit to your height or change the color of your hair?" But there is stuff inside you that works off your autonomic nervous system that *can* add a cubit to your height or change the color of your hair; and ladies deal with that stuff more than men do because they are part of the birthing cycle. At some birthings I've seen flesh stretch in such a way that I had to believe that there's a little magic in it; I've seen tissue change state from quite solid to something malleable, under the stress of some glands. That's really pretty fancy. And some of the stuff is just too heavy for you to control with your conscious mind, so your unconscious mind controls it—just like your digestive system. Everybody's stomach does chemistry, but if your brain had to figure it out first, you'd die of indigestion.

That earlier use of the word elemental doesn't relate to this. When I say ladies are an elemental force, I mean it in the same way the wind is an elemental force. Originally the elements are earth, air, fire, and water. And wind is an elemental force; tide is an elemental force; volcanoes are elemental forces: stuff that moves just like tides and earthquakes, that no man can do much about. Better to don't try, better to make peace with it.

(Q.: What if the elements are against you and there is always one force that out-fences you and is always one step ahead of you?) This is just like the story about the fellow who went to the Zen Master and said he was troubled by some ghost that kept bugging him. And the Zen Master told him what to do. The next time the ghost came to see him, he reached down into this jar by his bed and he got a handful of soybeans and he said to the ghost, "How many beans in my hand?" It's like when I'm dreaming sometimes, I'll dream that I'm going to read a book that I haven't read before, and I can tell how stoned I am by whether it's something I haven't read before, or whether the dream falls apart at that point because I haven't got any information to put in a book that I haven't read before. Try to fool your head?

(Q.: What about regrets and remorse?) Well, there's regrets

and remorse, and there's knowledge of bad karma, which are different things. Regrets and remorse are you wish you'd done better, maybe for the sake of your ego. Knowledge of bad karma is knowing you should have done better for the sake of your soul. Well, that's a little stronger spur than the other kind.

(Question.) She says that she'll be talking about anger without putting it on other people, but that she holds it in and bottles it up and it gets her nutty that way. I noticed by the tone of your voice when you spoke to me that you don't speak as forcefully or as truthfully as you feel—you speak softer and like a little girl, so that you don't impose yourself on anybody, and all the time you are being like that, you are feeling inhibited, which makes you mad. And if you learn to take your voice out of that range up there so it can really vibrate your throat chakra, so it comes Ahmmm with confidence from your stomach as it comes out, and speak fully and freely as you feel and don't use a little high voice like that, you'll be closer to where you really are and you won't find yourself artificial and out of balance, being a way you aren't.

(Question.) That just means that vibrations move more slowly than the material plane does. Vibrations flow. They're a little thick, and they flow. And if you get into a very physical kind of lovemaking, you can get yourself off on a purely material orgasm before you've had enough vibrations to collect to where you can feel them yet. So you're supposed to go slow enough, and be gentle enough and self-aware of what it is you're really feeling—so you can feel the presence and the electricity coming on after a while. But you have to be patient, and remember what you're doing; you can't let yourself head-trip or think about what-you-should-have-said-to-the-man-who-came-into-the-Gate-today, or that nail you hit your thumb on. You have to be thinking about here-and-now, and feeling what is to be felt, and composing yourself just like you were meditating. Compose yourself to a pure, clean place, and then you can start feeling some energy. Then, when you start feeling some energy, you may have to give it a little help to keep it going every now and then, but sometimes you'll get it flowing so well and so smooth that you don't have to do anything physically anymore. You can just be still and move energy. The energy at that place is subtle, and if you're doing anything gross you'll mask it so you won't find it.

(Q.: How do you know knowledge of bad karma?) Well, knowledge of bad karma is when you know for sure that you did something that you have to do better than. And then you have to change your act. You have to find out why you be that way. Do you get angry because you care about stuff that doesn't happen, or because you build up and explode, or what? Are you introspective enough to know? You have to be very careful about caring about stuff. That's what makes people like clerks and people that are very officious and hard on people—like in the driver's license bureau or something, sometimes you find clerks that really want to be a way, and really care, and they are very fussy about it and they make everybody who passes through them have to go through that change. What happens to me as I get older is that I don't demand to be directing it; I don't even care about directing it. I'll be ready to watch it go to its normal conclusion and let it happen—you can't stop stuff from happening the wrong way, so you can try to make it happen the right way; and if you turn yourself into a little cartoon running around here and there, trying to direct it, you lose your strength and your power and your juice, and you get to where you can't do anything, because you devalue yourself. You have to be able to say, "Well, this is going to happen. I should probably just step back out of the way." Then if it wasn't cool, you can tell the folks from a better position and you can say, "Look what happened, and now you have to do better than that," but if you're always out there trying to stop it from happening, then you just start slipping your clutch and you can't stop it from happening. The world's going to go on with you or without you. They'll recycle you back into the system.

(Q.: What leads to self-deception?) Self-deception is stuff like telling yourself you were cool when you weren't. You can tell yourself you're cool when you weren't because your ego doesn't want to say you weren't cool. The person who's in that kind of place can rarely admit, in the here-and-now, in the transaction, that they were wrong. They have to fight it out, stop the transaction, go away somewhere and cool off for a while, and then come back and admit they were wrong. That's because they deceive themselves to such a point that in the midst of the action they are unable to say, "Well, I was wrong." Another kind of self-deception is to tell yourself that something you want to do—because you like to do it—is cool because you want to do it. That's another level of self-deception.

(Q.: In dealing with children, isn't it good to get angry? At least you're being honest.) No, angry is not the way you really are. Did you ever study Spanish? Okay, in Spanish they have two verbs, *estar* and *ser,* and they are both verbs *to be.* But one of them is to be permanently, forever, decreed, fated, that's the way it is. And the other one is, this is how you are right now in this time-frame, passing through, but you're probably going to change. And there are certain things you don't say one way or another. Like, by using the wrong verb form, you can make a difference in how you say it, of whether someone's going to get well or not. And anger is one of the temporary conditions. It is also volitional. You have to turn it on. It knocks on the door, but you have to open the door and let it in. And you have to say "No," when it knocks at the door. But you have to be self-aware enough to catch it at the place where it knocks at the door.

You have to make a moral judgment and say, "Anger is lethal." Anger is like poison. It has effects on people like radiation or strychnine, and if you do it to people it has those effects on them. And you have an obligation to no more unleash that on somebody than you would walk up and, say, punch them in the mouth. In fact, you can do more damage to somebody with your vibrations and your anger than you can by walking up to them and punching them in the mouth.

The classical teaching on that is Jesus' teaching where He said, "The prophets of old say unto you, *Thou shalt not kill;* but I say unto you, *Thou shalt not be angry with thy brother."* He says, "For if a man lust after a woman in his heart, it is the same as if he commit adultery with her." And that's a whole integrated teaching about how what you do in your heart of hearts, and your mind, and psychically, is real stuff and has real effects which you are responsible for—not in the sense that you're responsible to the driver's license people for your driver's license, but in the sense that if you paint yourself blue, you're going to be blue. You are the one who is changed by giving vent to those actions.

88

Really it's the question of what will is for. Some folks think that will is for getting what they want. A tycoon of industry uses his will to get what he wants. Will is powerful, but that isn't what you use it for. What you use will for is to don't be angry. What you use will for is to don't throw anything damaging into the situation, to leave the situation as clean as possible in order that you can look at it cleanly.

Children are very simple. If you get angry at a child, a child will get angry at you. If I see kids on the Farm who have a lot of anger, I think that somebody's been angry with them a lot or they wouldn't be angry a lot. It's taught. We teach our children by how we be, what it's okay for a grown-up to do.

(Question.) No, no, he says there's a danger of becoming a shallow person by mimicking what you should be. I didn't say to act like you're not angry when you're angry. I said to *don't be angry;* and it requires will of the order that John Paul Getty used to corner the market for the money he made; it requires the kind of will that an Olympic weightlifter puts out. It ain't hard to do. You can do it. And the more you do it, the better at it you get, just like anything else.

God Bless you all. See you next week.

August 22, 1976

Some folks say they would like to be a teacher on the Farm. "I'd like to teach the kids," or "Do the kids have any intellectual life?" Well, it's about imagination. There's a kind of kid's book that's supposed to be all about imagination; it has clever cartoons and stuff like that. And people say if you don't give the kids enough of the clever cartoons, you're depriving them of something. Well, you are—*someone else's imagination.* Not only are they someone else's imagination, they are some-

one's quick and hurried imagination. A kid's imagination is as good as any imagination; and what you want to do is give it good building blocks to imagine with. So, you won't raise your kids on cheap kid books out of the five-and-ten with somebody's old commercial imagination. When you're talking a-bout imagination, you're not talking about a cartoon, or something ephemeral. You have to understand that when you're talking about imagination, you're talking about *bringing something into being in your mind and having a clear enough vision of it and understanding it in all its parts well enough that you can bring it about into reality.* And if you have a cheap, hurried vision, if you have a cartoon vision, if you have a vision that doesn't have your full attention and love in it—if you have a vision that you do not put as much good time and attention into as if you were building a regulation outhouse, for example—then you will make a cheap vision; and when you try to bring it forth into reality, it will be complicated and messy and fuzzy, and it won't work right and you'll have to patch it up a lot—it'll be a low-quality vision, one of those visions it's hard to get anything to happen with.

Some people put all their attention into visions of stuff that only has about one chance in ten quadrillion of happening, claiming it's their artistic freedom. Well, when you're talking about freedom of mind, you're talking about freedom of visions, for people to create their own visions and try to live them.

I like to study old Hindu visions and Tibetan visions and whatever, but the visions that are most interesting to me are the ones that we share and create here and now in this generation among us. *The Farm is really an attempt to fulfill those visions that we've all had.* And to the degree that there is an agreement among them, it will happen. And to the degree that there is not agreement, it won't happen. And there is a very sensitive and delicate point which you have to arrive at, because you do want enough agreement for it to happen.

A certain portion of your vision must be left blank and Holy. There must be a Void, an uncreated from which the created may come. Its structure, and Form, form an emptiness. The form is our shared vision, and we agree on some things pretty plainly: we very strongly agree about being collective, about being vegetarian, about a spiritual search being an individual thing that everybody must partake of, in order that they can share the whole birthright. We have a strong shared vision.

A friend of mine used to say, "Don't give me paisleys for psychedelics; give me candlelight and old silver." It's like Rembrandt. Deep and important, profound and heavy, not fast and pastel and easy to draw. All the colors that God uses. Now that was a lovely vision he gave me, with a lot of artistic freedom. The whole magazine industry of magazines and literature is based on shared vision; but when it comes down to doing the thing, it is not as easy. *The vision to be lived is a lot more complicated; but we're living a shared vision.*

(Question.) Well, the thing Suzuki meant by that was that he wasn't in competition for being the best Zen Master around; he was just trying to take care of business. It would have been silly for him to have been in a contest about who's the best Zen Master, anyway. It's silly for any Zen Master to do it. It's silly for any Zen Masters to cop that they are different from any other Zen Masters even to the extent of one of them being better than the other; because it's an article of faith that no Bodhisattva who is a true Bodhisattva will tolerate any speck of unreal individuality, because it muddies up the nature of the Oneness of all of us. So I don't think it's like that. He tried hard. He died trying.

(Q.: What is the seventh sense?) The seventh one is clairvoyance, and the eighth is clairaudience. The sixth one is compassion, which the classical Greeks called the common sense. They don't mean horse sense, they mean the integration of all the senses into a commonness of perception that is what they call the sixth sense.

One of the common things that happens to people when they get stoned on psychedelics is synesthesia, or crossover senses. The senses are not that differentiated anyway: your eyes are just evolved out of skin; and your skin has a lot of light sensitivity. We're not really that differentiated. We tend to think that way because we have eye-ear-nose-and-throat specialists who tell us that we're all separate and charge us money for each part; but we aren't really that differentiated. If you find yourself feeling synesthesia, it's a clue that you're stoned and you ought to watch your step.

(Question.) The thing in the *Bible* where it says, "Resist not evil, do good"? Evil isn't anything except what you give it. As far back as St. Augustine and even previous to him, they pointed out that good has an intrinsic existence and that evil doesn't. Because good can be in it for the sake of good only, but evil is in it for the money, for the power, for the social position, for nice sexual partners and stuff like that. Evil is not in it for the sake of evil. No one is ever in evil for the sake of evil. Ego gratification, money; but not the sake of evil. So evil doesn't exist except insofar as people put their energy into it at that level. It has no separate existence other than what is carried in the minds of mankind. To the extent that something is good, it can exist; because nothing exists that is not good; because it's all a part of God.

So you should put your energy where it's going to come back to you. It's like playing music against a wall where the music comes back and you can hear it, or just playing out into an emptiness where it just goes and doesn't come back and you don't know. The United States is the way it is right now on account of resisting evil. We came up against the gestapo and the Nazis—and we learned from them. I just pray that we never have a choice to make like World War II in our lifetime. I just really pray.

I love you all a whole lot. God Bless you. Good morning.

July 18, 1976

Wakan ~ Holy

The concept of *Wakan*—Holy—has been on my mind lately, because the *Wakan* is what the Hopis are trying to prove to the government. The Hopis say, "We're trying to explain to you how we feel about Hopi land. It's like our Jerusalem. Can you understand that? It's Jerusalem for us Indians in this area, and that's why we don't want you to come and do a strip mine on it." They're trying to tell Congress that it is Holy, *Wakan*. That's interesting because that word is used among the Indians all up and down both continents to mean Holy. It is a strong and universal concept, and one that our culture lacks; our culture just doesn't have that piece of information to a sufficient degree. But there are a lot of people who understand something about *Wakan*—the millions of folks doing some kind of a spiritual thing, trying to grow, trying to learn to get better, all across the world there are people who know something about it. But if we believe that something is indeed *Wakan* how much weight or how much value do we put on that, in relationship to other things like making a living?

We try to pay attention to that; but even at that, we don't sometimes. There is stuff that I have resisted in a way that people think that I am the most conservative thing—stuff like 110-volt electricity going farther and farther into the Farm. I fought every pole that was put up, down all the way through this Farm. Every extension of electricity had to be justified as to "Why do we have to do that? "Do we really have to do that?" If you are talking about buying farm land, we were had; only about three hundred acres of this is farm land, and there are 1,400 acres of blackjack oak. But what we bought here was the chance to be the last piece of property out at the end of the road. A lot of hippie places are up canyons—we had one up a canyon once, with fifteen acres; one acre was flat—that was the driveway and the house, which is the trouble with buying one back up a canyon. But this is back out at the end of the road, and over that way there are twenty-five miles of oak trees. It isn't just the oak trees—some acorns are good to eat, but most of these are too bitter. *We came out here because we wanted to be out in the boondocks to find some room to get Holy.*

It's funny because it's just an accident that we have the language we have: it would be equally justifiable for a lot of folks I know, if they modified their language, to say, "Man, did we get Holy last Saturday night! Shoo—we got so Holy." Well, isn't that what we are trying to do? Trying to get high. What's high? Is high a buzz? Zzzzzzzzz, that isn't high; that's just your organism saying, "Hey, there is something weird in here." We want to have *changes in consciousness,* and there are things that we have to do to have changes in consciousness.

If you are playing an electric guitar and you want to play a little feedback, you start walking up to the amplifier with the guitar, and the feedback starts getting louder and louder. If you can see inside the amp, as that feedback gets louder and louder, the tubes in the amp start glowing brighter and brighter: as you get right up to it and just pour right into it, they go from orange up to yellow and they get almost white. They really glow—that's why feedbacking too much isn't good for your equipment, because you are actually heating it up real hot, and the electron streams are pouring really strong and it's just really glowing—and the aura of the amplifier increases  a great deal during that time—it's revving itself.

Well, that's meditation. You take your instrument of attention and feed it back into your amplifier until you get high. That's cool—that's good, because the idea is that once you get it revved up, you are going to get smart enough to figure it out, smart enough to make big decisions. *That's why a lot of teachers say, "Get high," instead of "Be good," because they want you to be good; but they have been arguing with people all their life and they have found that people don't be good when you say, "Be good," but if they get high, sometimes they say, "Ohhh." It is the most scientific form of social work in psychology that you could possibly do, because it is based on the idea that you come to each person, and you give them some form of operation they can perform, and then they can make their own observation, and they can discover the Diamond Jewel in the Lotus, if they try hard enough.* The Diamond Jewel in the Lotus is reality as it really is.

Also, besides when you are feedbacking, your tubes light up just when you play strong, too. You don't have to feed it back on yourself. That's okay to do for a while, to rev your equipment up, but you also pour it to other folks, and that revs it up;

and if you give it to someone else who understands, they give it back. What we are supposed to be doing here is to be like a hothouse of vibrations, like a collector. In the greater society, people's bad deeds travel a long way these days. Before the world had all these airplanes and fancy communications, local dictators could be ignored—to be sorrowed over but ignored— but now we can't do that anymore, because it's all connected: the deeds that people do cause karma that causes karma, . . . the original people don't know what they did to cause that karma.

Just now, this far down the line, one of the biggest advertising agencies in New York says, "We feel that the effect of our advertising which has been to sponsor violent shows on television is causing so much social disorder that it is costing us money." No kidding. Somebody figured it out, that they just can't pump that stuff out all the time without it coming back; and one of the biggest agencies is saying they aren't going to sponsor violence anymore, because they are realizing that it does come back on them. For fifteen or twenty years, all the psychologists have been trying to tell them about that. Well, in one of the big network offices that we were in in New York, one of the executives had been mugged in the executive washroom—in the executive washroom itself.

The Farm is an intense little hothouse society, and if we put out ego or anger into this society, it might not bounce around quite as much, but it is going to bounce around some. You come through here and you look around, and you say, What a lot of nice smiling faces, what a lot of good-looking folks—healthy, good skin, nobody sick—good-looking people; and sometimes I think I might be the only one that knows that some of them are carrying ten or twelve other folks, and some of them are being carried; and nobody knows, because it isn't relevant. We make it. If we put out good vibes into that interacting, reactive, instantaneous feedback that is the mind of the Farm, if we put out the best stuff we can, that feeds back around and carries us. The real thing that makes the Farm work, is right in your own heart of hearts where you have to decide that if that kid bugs you one more time, you are not going to get mad, but you are going to do something creative instead.

There are husband and wife teams here in which one of them is pushing on the other one to change them, "You have to change, you have to change,"—and they don't change. This is a fairly common one. If you are going to be that way with someone, you have to really think over your relationship with this person that you are married to. Marriage gives you the license to a certain degree of intimacy in the eyes of the greater society—like the old story about the people that got the hunting license instead, and the clerk hollers, "Don't do it, 't'ain't for it." A lot of people think having been opened into this degree of intimacy also means that they get to be not-very-nice to the other person sometimes. Or you have the case that happens with the couple that's courting, and they treat each other so good and be so nice to each other, and then they get married. In a fair amount of time it's about, "You don't help out with the dishes," or something like that. This is what a place like the Farm has to make one of its prime yogas. The person living in the house with you who bugs you, you'd better come to terms with; you can't be cynical about what it is we're doing here.

I want to toughen up the fiber that the Farm is woven out of. As a piece of weaving, we're working on it all the time—the farming happens and we clear land, and we plant the food. Changing the land around is like the weaving of the fabric; but the thread that it's woven out of is your individual heart, and whether you are cynical to any degree. What I find as the weakness in our fiber—I guess I can even say moral fiber, it's an old saying—is that we aren't studying our individual paths as hard as we should be. People call me up quite a bit for help about something; and most of the time when somebody calls me, what I tell them is what they already know. Sometimes I think of the old story about the teacher who said, "I've been sitting here by the river selling water for all these years; and people have been buying water from me rather than dip it out of the river."

When China made the jump that it made—from scaring everybody twenty-five years ago because they thought China was going to be so poor they would jump off and rip off all the people in the world just for food—it was like growing a giant

mugger next door scaring everybody. But instead, they learned to feed themselves. And they didn't start and go through the same changes the U.S. did; they didn't go through a pioneer, old-fashioned kind of trip: they started off at the level of technology that they could borrow from the rest of the world right there on the spot— at the state of the art, which is the only way they could have made it.

That's what we've got to be like; we have to start out at the state of the art. We're going to hook up the Farms with tele-type for constant information exchange, because we flow information from one Farm to another all the time. We grew to a level in San Francisco where we were really strong in the city and couldn't get out—nobody knew us outside of San Francisco. Meeting with two thousand people once a week is humongous, that's outrageous; it was outrageous at the time, and it would be outrageous if anybody were doing it today—but

it didn't get out of the city until we did. We came here, and then we got to be national. When we were first here we really communicated with San Francisco a lot because it was our base where we had come from. Now we don't really communicate a lot more with San Francisco than we do with Florida, Michigan or New York or something; but we became national by going halfway across the country and then communicating with our friends on the other end. And now we are national, and even international, and we need to get massively international. How many folks do you figure that, if they found a way to do it in their country, would do this? Really a lot of folks would like to be in a successful community. Why is it a successful community? To be international, we have to be able to go from a national base; and that's why all the Farms have to be able to move as one, that's why we are going to hook up teletype and stuff like that so we have a national base, a broader base of support so that when we go to other places we will actually be representatives from a broad base from across the country so that we can actually say that *we represent something from the country,* that we ain't just like a few people who sold the Indian lands while the rest of the Indians didn't want to do that, but that we're coming from a broad base of support.

The only reason church and state are separated is not because it is more efficient—it is actually less efficient—it's that you can't leave any absolute power laying around, because statistically it may go through several hands and be cool, but eventually somebody will pick it up and misuse it; so we have separation of church and state. But other than that, I can't separate what we are doing spiritually and politically—I mean the real politics of the world is people traveling back and forth from country to country and carrying true information and true scoop, which is how people are learning what's really going on in other countries.

The people are developing a planetary consciousness in spite of modern communications, not because of it. The big heavyweight media don't foster world communications. The Russians got the Olympics and they were going to charge the networks such a high price for filming the Olympics that the networks had to back out. Why is there enough money in who's going to televise the Olympics to move all three networks—which is like the fourth arm of the government of the U.S.—and the

Russian government to get nose-to-nose hassling over that power? *There is such a tremendous magnetic attraction by the people of the world to know what is going on with the other people of the world, that's why.* And the Olympics was one of the things set up by the people of the world to try to make a world thing happen: it was the Olympic athletes themselves who elected to mix themselves up into a large group not separated out by country, and do a circuit of the field themselves as the athletes trying to represent everyone.

We don't have a real world government, but we have bits and pieces of it. We have world weather information; we don't lie to the Russians about what clouds are going to go across their territory, they don't lie to us about that; it would be silly. Then there's some other funny things happening. Eight Liberian tankers have been in trouble in twenty-five days. Now some people think that the reason for that is some kind of Bermuda Triangle type trip, some heavy mystical thing; but what's happening is the Universe telling us something about Liberian tankers: that Liberia has the lowest standards of registry of any country in the world, and all the cheap-o outfits register with them. That's why the tankers that go down are Liberian tankers because they are the cheapest tankers there are—the oldest, rustiest, worn out, crude, no-life-boat-equipment man-traps.

Liberia and Panama do that, front out boats that aren't safe, as a cottage industry to make money for the country. Compare that level of cooperation with the international weather service as different levels of how countries can cooperate. The amount of money that Liberia and Panama make out of that is negligible compared to the damage caused by the oil that is being dumped on the coasts of the world.

Wakan is worthless in that game—there *is* no *Wakan* in that game, nobody's, not yours or anybody else's. The Hopis are saying, "Look, the government may be atheistic, the government may be agnostic; that's cool, it's the government, nobody cares. But we, some of the people of the world, have a little bit of land." Not much—there is only five thousand people and it's mostly rocks and desert and high buttes and stuff, mostly who lives there is rattlesnakes—but when they talk about Jerusalem, they say that when the angel that was building the world was flying over Israel, the bottom dropped out of the sack he was carrying his rocks in. It isn't much, but it is their Jerusalem.

That is one of the things you have to recognize: that it goes right to the level of deciding whether you're going to get heavy with your wife—if you come and try to intimidate her into doing something for you, you are damaging the *Wakan,* and millions of people are paying attention to what we are doing, and are vitally interested in this experiment—wondering whether they are going to spend the rest of their life in an old folks' home. In the greater society, if you have a child that you don't think is sufficiently cute or smart, you send him away to an institution, where you send your old folks—there's that world going on out there; and then there is this one. There are a lot of folks who say that the only thing wrong with this one is that they don't know if it's going to last or not. "I'd really hate to come and invest everything into it and then find myself sixty or eighty years old and have the thing fold up and leave me with nothing to do." It's scary, right? The only thing that helps those people is for us to come on hanging-in-there, year after year after year. That's the only thing that will give those people the courage to join us—people who are betting on us, who love us, who think that we are the hope, and are afraid to mess with us, because it's only been a few years, gotta watch 'em a little longer, gotta watch 'em a little longer. And everything that we do here as individuals affects that message that is sent out to the world, of, "Can you do it? Can you do it?"

In Tennessee, there is a state law against cutting through stream beds. Well, right now there is a big strip-mining company that wants to do ten thousand acres in Tennessee and they are going to cross maybe six or eight creeks in the course of it. And the environmentalists are saying that if they divert all those creeks—the real problem is all those minerals being released from all those rocks being scrambled around; that the stream is going to be really thick downstream. It's going to wash a lot of stuff out of that soil for years and years. It won't be the same creek: it might be too thick for fish to live in, even—sulfuric acid and stuff like that comes out of strip-mining waste.

That's right here in Tennessee, and what that's about is the standard of living of the U.S. Most of the energy we use is translated out of coal, or oil. As Bucky Fuller says, there is enough energy used to maintain this standard of living as if each one of us had two hundred slaves that were capable of working twenty-four hours a day in all weather, at greater levels of precision and strength than we are capable of— that's how much energy it takes to maintain the American standard of living. Well, having somebody off in another country working for a dollar a day that you don't even have to look at him and whip him and you get the results of his work, is another kind of slave.

Oil is not being replenished. The costs of the amount of sunlight energy and animal energy and vegetable energy that goes into producing a gallon of gasoline is thousands and thousands of dollars per gallon, if you look at the real energy; that's not an economical energy source. We are going to use that up; we have to do better.

Two or three couples have left the Farm recently, saying it isn't warm enough, the food isn't good enough,

something like that. Well, it *is* warm enough, and the food *is* good enough; but also, according to the greater standard of the world, *we are fat.* I don't mean we're making it; I mean we are fat. But what we are doing here is not just a hippie old folks' home. Anybody that thinks this is a hippie old folks' home should go move back to their mother's. If you don't like something here or you don't think that it is up to good enough standards, your duty as a citizen is to *change it*—not to split. There are folks on the Farm for whom, for reason of age or health, we want to have a certain level of plushness—electricity and stuff. That's good to do that. And we are probably not going to have outdoor outhouses someday; we're probably going to have indoor composting ones, where you get to be warm in the inhouse.

But that isn't what it is really about. What it is really about is that this is a really dedicated, devoted revolutionary spiritual movement being based out of here, and you are expected not just to be making it or surviving, but if you're not already in a condition to carry a lot of  mail, you're supposed to be polishing your act—getting yourself together so you can carry a lot of mail, because all you folks are going to have to carry a lot of mail, and you aren't very many people at all.

We have an amazing amount of influence for no bigger than we are. There are towns in Guatemala ten times as big as ours, with no world influence at all. The Americans think that we're poor; and our village has more stuff than a village ten times its size in another country—that gets into powers and powers, ten-times-that-times-the-next-one. It gets into incredible waste. We don't know yet what is the proper level to do this at; we are trying to learn it as we go. We're not trying to be doctrinaire, and we're not coming out of *a priori* material plane assumptions. We have some *a priori* spiritual assumptions, such as, "We are all One," but having a lot of *a priori* material assumptions gets you into trouble. Bucky says if you want to play his particular intellectual game, you have to give up hearsay. You have to give up all that unreliable evidence, and collect your own evidence from what's going on in front of you, or you aren't going to get to know what's really going on.

We do something like a social *sadhana*—our path is the path of the community, and not just the individual; it is the path that a whole community can walk together. So everything that you do in the community is part of the path. The way everybody gets their food, is all about how we are really One. It's not conceptual about being One. To not be cynical and to really do the thing is a path; and if you be honest with the path, that path will do things to you. This is not a holding place; we did not come here for this to be the elephant's graveyard. Down the line we are going to have to take as much pains as the Hopis do to keep from getting over-civilized. We

are going to be so popular, have so many people want to see us, get so noticed and have so much publicity— we are going to have to be very careful to not get civilized out, and to remember our thing. Some people wonder, and say, "When did God say to grow long hair?" Well, what long hair is for on the Farm is to keep your ears warm; but off the Farm what long hair is for, is to keep you from getting any airs or ideas of social position—to remind you where you're at and who you are. It's a very helpful part of our yoga; you never know when you are going to get a little teaching at that level.

We are voluntarily assuming the level of existence that other people in the world could aspire to, but that is not our real power: our real power is a lot more than that. We don't wear jewelry, for example, because jewelry is a collection of wealth; but we wear pretties, we wear all this nice embroidery—you can do somebody out to the limit for about five dollars, out to where you can't look at them. And that's what the poor people do all over the world, is they make their pretties, and what's valuable in them is their labor. But jewelry is an accumulation of wealth. Really, the reason anyone wears a diamond ring is that they think, "I'm so rich I can carry a thousand dollars on my hand, and not pay any attention to it." We don't cut

our hair because the only people that care if you cut your hair is

the army and businesses and people like that; and one of the things I'm symbolizing by having hair this long is that I obviously haven't worked for the military or industrial complex in a long time. I'm different from the one I used to be, way different. I used to wear Brooks Brothers suits, just like in the old poem about, "There you go in your damn, damn Brooks Brothers suit," by Rexroth. Well, I was there in my Brooks Brothers suit. I lost that suit in British Honduras, and it floated around

in trunks in Central America for many years; and then I got it back. By that time I wasn't wearing that kind of suit anymore, and I gave it to the Goodwill right away. Somebody said, "Wouldn't you want to have one good suit, in case you had to talk to the President or something?" If that was the condition, I wouldn't talk to the President. It says that you are limited from certain things by growing long hair. Good.

That is not to say that the Farm is not without honor for individuals that can distinguish themselves; the individuals that distinguish themselves on the Farm are honored. We aren't into things like testimonial dinners or gold watches or calling them long Sanskrit names, but we know who is packing it and they are always respected. But as far as any worldly social position goes, we have an obligation to be certain that we don't by accident accept any of it, or we could become so compromised that the real poor people in the world—because we are imitation poor people—the real poor people of the world would tell right away if we were selling out, maybe getting a steak on the side while we said we were going to eat with them.

I think one of the main things is that the individuals are going to have to grow up to be trustworthy enough to handle a lot of energy for a lot of other people, and you folks . . . Who else? Do you think I'm going to go out and hire some specialist from Nashville to do my heavy stuff? This is an out-front invitation to growth, not just for us, because we're already fat and sassy and got it made. Anybody who goes home to the flush toilets because they can't hack it here is just cowardly. That's what I believe in my heart of hearts. Sure, you can cut your hair; sure, you can go home to flush toilets; sure, you can go back to college; you can do any of that stuff, and put your foot right smack back on the neck of a bunch of peasants that are starving all over the world. This is not a drill: this is reality. The Diamond Jewel.

Good morning. God Bless you.

January 9, 1977

The Theory and the Practice

What I'm going to talk about this morning is the theory and the practice. The theory is that if we behave in truth, as if we're all One, that we'll get to know something about Oneness. And Oneness is about God. In theory, we get along so well together, that we're able to live in close quarters and have the advantage of a great deal of synergy. Synergy is one of Bucky's words. It means if you put a bunch of ingredients together there's going to be new advantages and new energy sources that are going to be a resultant of that mixture that cannot be predicted ahead of time. It isn't that Bucky doesn't believe in the first three laws of thermodynamics; it's just that he doesn't think they include the human factor as an accurate statement of the situation: that we're all going to get smarter and learn how to use it better and faster than we lose it when it's running down. That's the theory; that we understand our Oneness, we understand what it is we're doing here.

I had a reporter hit on me one time with "What drives you?" I said, "I ain't driven, I'm driving." Now some of you even understand that we actually know what we're doing here.

Except for certain wild eccentricities, the theory around the world from religion to religion, teacher to teacher, is pretty much standard. What I've noticed from catching the weather news the last couple of days is that when it gets really cold and really bad and the chips are really down, we're better off here than in the city. Far out. Weren't you glad you had an ax and a wood stove—instead of trying to figure out how.to get yourself some natural gas from Texas?

The theory is that we're all going to take care of all of us and we aren't going to leave any of us out. And that nobody's going to have better housing and food and medical and all of the basic things which we add to life, liberty, and the pursuit of happiness as givens for humans.

Another particular teaching we share with Mr. Fuller is that we have to get rid of the idea that one has to *earn a living:* we get to live here, and then we all work as hard as we can to do what we can do, but not from the basic idea that your right to live and exist on this planet has to do with your job. We're just going to break that. There's a lot of feelings like that we're trying to break—I was just talking to Paul about being over in medical school in Memphis: it's so wild to not be in it for the money. He's getting to study medicine and not be in it for the money. Almost without exception, the vast, vast majority, way out into the ninetieth percentile of people in medical school are doing it for the money.

And that we tell the truth. That's some more of the theory. We tell the truth, and those among us who have good vision and courage help out all the rest of us well enough that no one gets intimidated and that no one gets to intimidate anyone; and we give up intimidation as a manner of making decisions. Now there are whole levels of society where what they consider the usual confrontation between management and labor is a contest of intimidation. One side says, "We'll quit working, and you'll lose money so fast you'll want us back." And the other side says, "I'm fat enough, I can let you starve." Isn't that what labor relations come down to? It's just a question of saying, "Okay, if you're going to go off and jump downhill, I'm so much fatter than you that you'll starve before I do." Theory of capital, basically. Theory of community is that we not be competitive about the groceries. We be pretty good about that. But the idea is that we're all going to be high enough and spiritual enough that we are going to be good to each other to make it be good for everybody.

That's at the theory level and the level of the ideals—and then there's the level of how well we are doing it— right across the board: how well are we really taking care of each other? I could name three or four ladies who have been close to leaving the Farm in the past couple of weeks because they felt they weren't being covered—and when we checked into the situations, sometimes we found they weren't. I could, and I even might, name several men who still think it's all right to intimidate a lady just because you're married to her. And the advice I've been passing out on that, I'd like to make public to the Farm. If you feel a necessity to intimidate your lady, go do it to someone else's wife and *see what it gets you.* Maybe that will help clear up the nature of the situation in your mind as to what it's really about. And as Ina May has said over the telephone to several men in the last few weeks, "I am morally certain that you wouldn't treat your lady that way if you weren't bigger than she is." This is the level of how do we really take care of ourself. The reason I'm talking about this is I'm following the instructions given in the *Bible.* I have talked to these folks privately a lot of times. And so now I bring it up in front of the witness of the church, in order that everyone may have the nature of the agreements clearly established in their mind.

I've been gone for a while and I've been getting my juice back, and it's just begun to come back. I could really tell when it came back—you know when the energy's there and when it isn't. It seems to me that when I go on the road and I'm not in evidence for a while a certain level of thing comes up: people doing stuff to other people they wouldn't do if I was around. If there are people doing stuff to other folks when I'm not around that they wouldn't do if I was around, it means that no one is naive and silly and young and idealistic enough to stand up and be Mighty Mouse when I ain't here. If stuff like that goes down when I'm not around, where is Mighty Mouse? Where is he? I thought he lived in all our hearts.

I had a really good meditation this morning. It was one of the kind where I needed it like a bath, and I was so grateful to get to do it. I thought, "I'm just going to relax and really take it easy," and just sat down and didn't even try to sit up in zazen for the first ten or fifteen minutes—I just kind of folded my hands and let them hang in my lap and didn't even try to sit up too straight. I sat there and let my head run across what it wanted to—I just sat for a while without forcing anything, and began to get some good rushes; and then I started to straighten up. I got it on pretty good before the OM, but it really got clean in the OM. *Once a week we come here and do this thing: we pool our energy and we bring our energy up together.*

But it can't be a once-a-week hit. The place where we lose energy is through the cracks in our agreement. When we first came here we were really low on housing. Back in the first couple of winters, people had to be willing to move out of a house on a little while's notice. Somebody might be having a baby, or maybe getting sick, and would need a better level of shelter than they had; and somebody would just have to move; and we moved people around like musical chairs all winter to try to keep the old folks and the babies and the folks who needed it in good warm houses as much as we could. And now we're pretty fat and we have a lot of houses and a lot of people attached to where they live, and we've seized up a little—you can't move folks so easily anymore because they get attached, and they think that the houses are theirs.

The more I watch us run ourself the more I understand the country. I feel very compassionate with Jimmy Carter and where he's at right now. He's been trying for many years to get ahold of that handle, and now he wants to know how he's going to push it. In his campaign, he said he wants to do a lot of stuff; and now he's in office and the question is, can he do any of that stuff? Will anybody let him do any of that? Like give up plutonium power plants—he understands where they're at; he is a nuclear engineer who helped design atomic submarines, and he says those plants ain't safe. Boy, I'm grateful for him to have that attitude. But the question is can he do anything about it. And he may not even be able to do anything about it, because the country as we live in it, is a compromise. And it has to be a compromise, because there's nowhere else for the rest of the folks to go, so it has to be a compromise. And about the main success of the country is when we don't fall to civil war and killing each other. Just that we get to be a country this big, and claim ourselves as a country, when if it wasn't for modern communications and stuff like that, we could hardly keep track of this much territory.

During the Vietnam war there was a certain amount of respect accorded to the pacifist by everybody. And then after the Vietnam war, some people were willing to drop that and get down to the business that we were just longhairs again. Well, that was a moral force that the longhairs in this country had. They had a moral strength for what they were doing about Vietnam. Here on the Farm we have a certain moral strength that we *have* to do this thing. And we're trying to let folks know where it's at as they come to be with us, and we're pretty good in a lot of ways—we've been able to grow from two hundred and fifty people on this Farm to the thousand people that's on it now. But there's a question of standards—I fight for the standards. Fighting for the standards makes me understand Barry Goldwater. That's all he was really doing; he was fighting for what he figured were the standards.

How many ladies here truly and honestly—and don't be afraid to put your hand up here, because if you're afraid to put your hand up here, what are you going to do at home—how many ladies here think they get intimidated by their husbands? How about that? We have twelve or fifteen ladies here with a severe enough case that they'll snitch their old man off here in church. Well, the first thing this Farm has got to be, is free. Everybody that's here came here on their free will; they wanted to come here, and nobody here is supposed to get intimidated, not by groups, not by individuals, not by men or women, not by people with different kinds of job classifications—nobody gets to intimidate anybody to get anything to happen. Now you might think that it's just in cases of wife-beating that intimidation goes on. It's not; there was a level of intimidation going on between a couple of board members—one board member leaning on the other one to get more money, and the other one feeling pressured and pushed, because this other board member was applying pressure to him—not out of anything other than trying to make it for the Farm, to get up some food and pay some of our bills, but pushing. Well, if there is anybody pushing anybody in that scene it means that we aren't all walking in the same direction because that's the direction we thought was right. Shouldn't have to be anybody pushing anybody.

We're hand-selected really; we come from all over the United States, all over the world, hand-selected. It is not accidental that you're here; you followed a certain thing to get here. Heard there was something happening and wanted it to be true. Well, it's a good thing to hear about it, and it's a  good thing to want it to be true, and it's a good thing to want to live like it; but the other thing is where the taxes come in, about how willing are you to put out the juice to *make* it be true.

I had the good fortune to get a report of Governor Brown's state-of-the-State message, which was ten minutes long. The first five minutes dealt with economics, and the second five minutes he said, If you want to cut the government services any lower than they are, in order to lower the government spending, then what you have to do is to get up from in front of your television set and go out in the street and *take care of somebody who needs to be taken care of so it doesn't have to be done by the government*. The last thing that he said is, he told the California Legislature he had heard that they were considering reinstating capital punishment; and he said to don't even bother to bring it to him if they don't get a two-thirds majority because he's going to veto it anyway. Well, now, it's like that on the Farm. *I'll bet none of these ladies that feel like they were intimidated live out of reach of somebody on the Farm to ask for assistance in that case.* It's funny, but the kinds of things that make me understand what it's like to be a lady in this country and this world are things like having been in the Marine Corps and the penitentiary. I've felt what it was like to be under somebody's hand, anybody's.

I think what we need to realize about the theory and the practice is not that we necessarily stand in a circle and dance to the music of any particular language or nationality, or any-

thing; but that, just like the Sufis, we transmit *baraka*. Now *baraka* is what the Sufis call the energy that can flow between people. And Sufi dancing is fun, but the real object of Sufi dancing is that someone in the circle has some juice, and that as you dance, by going through similar motions and emotions and being together, that you become more similar and the energy can pass between you. And that's the way Sufi Sam, who was a very stoned old man, would go out and dance with folks and they'd get energy from it. And that's excellent if you live in a city. Pir Vilayat Khan does that, gets folks' juice up and gives his energy to them; he has plenty of juice, he gets me high.

Here we don't necessarily do it dancing in a circle, we do it dancing our life on this Farm.

Here are some of the things in our path. Rather than sit in a cemetery as a yogi to conquer your fear of death, you love everyone very much, and the odds are that you're going to lose one now and then; and you try to learn to don't fear death. And instead of sending a certain amount of money that you make at your job in tithing to help other people less fortunate than yourself, you dedicate *all your work* to those less fortunate than yourself. Dedicated to the all, to everybody, to work without attachment to the fruits of your labors. The path is not to head as hard and as fast as we can to the highest possible standard of living. We realize that there is a cutoff to the standard of living we are going to achieve, and that we ain't ever going to be rich gringos. And part of the path is if we have to be a little chilly, or maybe don't have any chili, whichever—part of the path is that you do your best, and you keep feeling good about it, and you hold up your end of the energy so that no one has to hold you up.

If there was no intimidation going on on the Farm, one person trying to throw out a little intimidation would be like a great red light going off, and everybody would say, "Wow! Look at that." If we didn't have any background radiation of a few husbands picking on their wives, we wouldn't have any intimidation on the Farm at all and nobody would be able to pull any off. Isn't that really where it's at? Or folks that ain't into changing anything—and it ain't even a question of being nice to their wife, it's just a question of that they've managed to be bad-tempered enough on the people of their household long enough that the people of their household are afraid to tell them anything because they're afraid that they'll get bad-tempered about it. Well, intimidation on the Farm is really un-sane; un-sane because you have the most help and the best chance to get out from under it here; this is where you're going to find the most people dedicated to not being that way.

The theory is what we're supposed to return to when we get snagged in the practice. What a lot of us do is we derive the theory and then we try to do the practice—and it gets kind of difficult, and we get square and hard and authoritarian and rigid and dumb. We have a whole bunch of really flexible, flowing, Gestalt, dynamic, hip ideals, and we should use them when it's difficult. Even though I don't recommend a twenty-minutes-a-day kind of meditation path, what our path is supposed to be like is that when you're out trying to do the theory and you run into a snag in the practice, then you sit down and shut up and listen to your heart for a while and try to remember why you're doing this, and why we are doing this together, and that we love each other, and that it's almost like getting married to be in a thing like this, because it's like joining a village. A village of a thousand people down in the middle of Mexico or India or somewhere might only have eight or ten blood-lines in it, and everybody might all be family, cousins and cousins throughout the whole town; in fact, that's how it usually is. That's how the natural-grown village ends up, and we're an artificial hothouse village, so we're growing this village. We have to just become cousins, don't we? Aren't we all cousins, anyhow? In New Mexico among the Mexican people, one of the things that you call somebody is *primo*—"Hey, *primo!*" Well, your *primo* is technically your first cousin. And your first cousin is really tight. They have a name for brother-in-law that's like that—*cuñado*. We knew a cat who was named Cuny because he was this family's *cuñado;* his entire identity was a *cuñado.* You guys are all my *primos* and *cuñados,* ain't you? Who else? I keep asking Margaret how come we have such weird friends; she says, "Don't nobody else like us."

If we don't keep the agreements, then the agreements fall apart. There's a thing between keeping the agreements and not getting so conservative as to be a hassle to people; and that's really a lot like driving a car on ice, and the Farm fishtails a certain amount pretty continually. Anybody who's been here long enough to see it knows that, and sees how the thing changes and changes; and they begin to see the parts that don't change, too. Yes, we're always going to come back and feed everybody, of course; yes, we're going to pay our bills; no, we're not going to burn anybody; we're going to keep the agreements that we made with the neighbors, the banks, and each other; and I don't see anything about success or failure in it. It seems that among us we can keep that agreement, if we choose to.

This is a spiritual thing. And we cannot solve our problems by materialistic ways of doing it. I hope it hasn't been devalued too much by the little yellow button with the smile on it and all that kind of thing, but *to put out good vibes will make us healthier and smarter and richer. If we didn't do anything else but improve our vibes, all the other stuff would improve too.* That's what it says in the *Bible,* really, about taking care of yourself and keeping yourself spiritually clean. Don't hunt after being rich; hunt after being spiritually clean. Once you get spiritually clean, everything else will fall on you. The religious idea that says you're supposed to be a slave here and that you'll get free in Heaven is *not at all true.* The way it really works is if your spiritual discipline works for you, *you will prosper now,* to the limit of karma: you're still going to catch an ice storm, or maybe the bridge will collapse under you, all that kind of statistical stuff; but basically if you do a good spiritual thing, you will prosper in other ways, too. It is not unreasonable, it's not magic. People like to do business with sane, healthy, happy people.

Anyway, the Farm is in really good shape for psychotic right now; we're hardly psychotic at all. We're a little neurotic, maybe it's just cabin fever from a long winter, but we're a little neurotic.

If you look in somebody's eyes who is psychotic you might start to hallucinate a little bit—somebody who is psychotic is really stoned and is having trouble coping with how stoned they are. You can change from being psychotic to knowing where it's at in one move, in one jump. Now neurotic is a head-trip; neurotic is thinking you're not fulfilling your expectations, or you're not fulfilling your daddy's expectations; or somebody thinks something about you, or you think that people are looking at you or you think that your nose is too big, and you think you'd be better looking if you didn't be fat or skinny or tall or short or blond or bald or whatever it is that bugs you. And being strung out on all that kind of stuff, and thinking about yourself instead of thinking about all of us and the greater body of the world, is being neurotic.

I'm very grateful to have the PLENTY project in Guatemala for that reason. Most of the classical stuff that anybody has for leverage on people, you all get for free on the Farm. Everybody gets to eat and everybody gets medical care and everybody gets a job, and all that sort of stuff, so there's no real leverage in anything. The theory that we're working under is that every one of us deserves food and health care and shelter, no matter what; but not everybody has to go to Guatemala for PLENTY, not everybody gets to go to foreign countries for PLENTY. I am going to use it frankly and blatantly for leverage on your gourd.

I really love you a whole lot, and I am completely aware that without you I would be standing here in the middle of an empty field without a greenhouse around me, talking to the weeds, without a microphone.

This is a real good time right now, this is a middle winter head, and we've never had a head this big and this strong in the middle of the winter before, this is fantastic. And if we really get it clean and make it clean like a small tight family . . . We just can't be full of complaining. Some folks come up to me, and I guess they know that if you come up and complain on me you don't get as good a stuff as you do if you don't, so they'll come up and lay a real nice one on me, and I hear a couple days later that they really unload on somebody, about what they really thought, that they didn't want to say to me or something. You better tell me what you really think, because I'm going to tell you what I really think, and wouldn't it be embarrassing if I did and you didn't?

Working with Spirit is like working with farming: putting the manure in the field and seeing the plants blossom and flower

is all part of farming; and talking the truth even if maybe it doesn't seem spiritual because it's so nitty-gritty about things, is like putting manure on the field. Let's grow a flower next year. We're starting here at a good place; let's grow a flower next year starting from here. Let's come on heavy. Good morning. God Bless you.

January 30, 1977

Making A Difference

I have had folks tell me that we weren't sufficiently new-age because we meet on Sunday morning—because meeting on Sunday morning was so traditional, and not sufficiently new-age. But there's a good reason for meeting on Sunday morning: this is the time when all our neighbors are meeting; all through here, for hundreds and hundreds of miles around here, there are churches full of people just about now. And once a prayer gets out through the roof of the church, God can't tell what kind of church it came from anymore; once it gets out through the roof of the church it's just out there. It is really strong to take this day and be part of that powerful and prayerful vibe, and to be in tune with our neighbors in the essence.

Now it's very strong and very stoned this morning, and really a good, clean, clear spiritual vibe. And there's a sort of level of teaching that I need to come back to again and again because we get new folks and because we bang our heads against the brick wall of Sangsara so much sometimes that we almost forget why we're doing it or how we're doing it or what it is we're doing or why we want to do this:

> *Attention is energy is Spirit is vibes is God is energy is Holy Spirit is life force, is, is, is, equals, equals, equals, nothing a computer would have any problem with.*

And we are all sources and transceivers of that energy: all of us are. If you are alive at all, you are a source and a transceiver of that energy—being a Republican does not bar you from being a source and transceiver of that energy.

The basis of our path is that if we always be faithful to that energy, that energy will keep us and sustain us and keep us smart enough so that we will be just and kind to one another: justice and liberty, goodness and kindness and all of the human virtues fall out of Holy Spirit. And we are as dedicated to the ends of justice as Tom Payne and Che Guevera, perhaps more so in that we think justice includes that

> *all people's lives are sacred;*

not just your political party or national group, or socio-economic peer group.

122

This energy follows a pretty straightforward set of rules, much the same as any kind of energy: you can accumulate it; you can modulate it; you can radiate it; you can send it and receive it.

Now the reason the Farm exists at this time is because enough people like us that they let us exist. The reason enough folks like us to let us exist is that on the average, not speaking in any absolute sense whatsoever, but on the average we tend to put out a sane and compassionate and inclusive vibration that doesn't seem to be going to be dangerous to any of the individuals involved. One considers what is the nature of the vibration we're putting out.

Somebody once pointed out that if you subtracted from the American population the thirty-five million grass smokers, about nine million in wheel chairs or retarded—body and mind assistance together—and the number of people in the penitentiary for some kind of crime, and you go on like that and take those people out and when you get done you don't know who's the Americans anymore, there isn't anybody left. Who is the silent majority? Who votes for somebody like Spiro Agnew? How does it happen, how come something as dumb as the entire Nixon/Watergate—at a national level of lying, breaking the oath of office, intentional subversion of the processes by which people are justly governed—how does this thing happen? And the entire Watergate investigation was looking for the mastermind, "Who is the evil genius who has done this?" Well, there ain't no evil genius that has done this. Evil by definition isn't genius; it's just disorganized, and Watergate/Nixon/etc. was the best that this country did at following the ideals that it says that it follows—of life, liberty, and the pursuit of happiness. It scared us sufficiently that maybe we're going to try to do better. It terrified the country when they saw how far out of control it got. Really out of control, no evil genius.

Now we say that the Farm is putting out this vibration of peace and love and good will into the world. We had forty ladies come to the intimidated ladies meeting; 4-0 not 1-4. Forty. Fourteen or so put their hands up in here last Sunday; the rest of them were apparently too intimidated to raise their hands at the meeting. And then we heard that besides forty that came to the meeting there were some who were too scared to come to the meeting because their husband might get mad. Forty ladies, that's eighty people, plus all their kids, plus all the people that are associated with them close enough that it uses up most of their time to go through that stuff. So who's watching the store? Who is the backbone of good vibrations that's holding the Farm together and keeping our intelligence and integrity at a high enough level that we're going to make a difference in the world? We're doing it somewhere around the corners—so far this well.

If you look through the population you can find some folks who seem more energetic than others; and the ways that you can tell if folks are energetic is by stuff like capability, happiness, self-actualization, intelligence, sense of humor, doing-their-number. You can tell that they have their energy on because they're doing their number. There's a certain amount of folks that need a jump-start now and then; we think that if we pool our energy, it'll average out stoneder for everybody: that we'll gain so much extra energy by pooling it that it'll be stoneder for everybody than everybody holding their own stash of energy. It's automatically assumed that the energy is free and open; and that gives us a certain viewpoint about things. You can take the eighty people plus families and kids and you haven't even gotten to the intimidated husbands yet, of which we have some. I'll tell you what: I maintain that this place is free; I maintain that this is the freest place you can find. You cannot check my statement while you are inhibited. If you want to find out how free it is you have to let yourself out. And I find that folks who are inhibited always assume that it's happening to them from the outside—that's one of the ways it works. We're on a group *sadhana*. That means that *one of our main obligations from living this close together is to don't intimidate or inhibit anyone else or inhibit their growth, or inhibit their ability to open their chakras, or any spiritual or intellectual heights to which they might be capable of climbing.*

One of the ways you can tell if somebody is into the juice is that when you bring the subject up, they say, "Who, me? No, not me." "Nope, never touch the stuff myself." And what makes the path here a possible kind of path, being this close together, is that there should be a high enough level of knowledge of energy and psychic technology that there ought to be a few people in any gathering on the Farm capable of following an energy transaction the way a fencing referee follows a fencing match. In fencing they come out with ch-ch-ch-chc and then one of them makes a point or something happens, and then the referee says that the action was carried from this side, there was a thrust here, there was a parry here, the riposte caused the action to go back the other way—he's able to explain what happened, ending up with a touch for this side. Well, we've been talking about this for ten years, it's been the subject one way or the other of most of the literature that's come out that we've done.

Truth is not a matter of majority. Truth is a matter of truth, not of a majority. But if you have a bunch of folks involved in something, you have a higher probability of there being at least one honest eyeball and one honest mouth in the situation, which can get you through a situation. *If you are pretty much in charge of yourself, you're capable of staying out of the energy and of allowing energy to be gathered somewhere, without feeling that you have to do something to it or about it.*

One of the reasons for the spiritual practice of non-attachment—trying not to be personally attached about your thing, or pain or whatever happens to you—is so that *you school yourself so that nothing can happen to you from the outside that can make you lose your energy, because as long as you have your energy on, you can do it.* I bring this up so strongly this morning because it's getting to be Spring and we're going to come into a strong season, and it's going to be heavy for everyone, which means that everybody has to be operating from really truly moral principles, nothing makeshift.

Now knowing why we do stuff is what makes us have good enough karma for us to survive this far, although we were probably some of the worst business people in the world. We walked into more dumb deals, got burnt more times, made ignorant deals, let our battleship mouth overload our rowboat tails numerous times; and it was just the strength of being spiritual and the strength of faith and the strength of being collective that made us strong enough, that made us be a smart enough dinosaur to plow through all of that and survive anyway. But we've got to come of age; we've been doing this for ten years. People are beginning to ask, "What is the state of your art?"

Somewhere back up in the tapes and the films is "the teachings," tons of teachings, just gangs of it. But that particular storage system of teachings, of tapes and typed transcripts and published books and all that kind of thing, is not the body of the teachings. The body of the teachings is how well they are understood in your mind and in the minds of everyone that I have communicated with in the last ten years since the days of Monday Night Class. It is a giant organic computer that has all of that information in it repeated many times and cross-indexed lots of different ways; and if there was enough of it scattered through this generation it will make a mark—it will make a widened circle of communication. If there's enough of it that enough people can hit on the essence of it, that it can continue and grow for a long, long time, we can leave a socio-spiritual, ecological legacy to the generations that follow us: something heavy to help out, if we create it clean enough now. And it exists in its most important form in your mind. No matter how poetically or aptly I may say something, unless someone can understand it and integrate it to the point where they use it in the next transaction, then it's just like up in the tapes, no more useful than that.

Now there is a tremendous body of information among you, hundreds of hours of shared communication about the nature of the mind and subconscious and the body and the energy and love and psychology; and if you don't interflow it among yourselves and test it in your daily life by testing things they say are supposed to work, and use them, then you are not using the teachings. Here's what I feel about the teachings: that they'll keep you sane. I think they'll keep you sane, no matter what the stress is that comes upon you, no matter what pain of mind or heart or body that comes upon you, it will keep you sane. So you should think in terms of the teachings. Now what are you learning? In what way can you control yourself better than you used to be able to do? In what way are you making any progress? Are you getting along with your old lady or have you guys been living the same movie day by day by day for ten years and haven't changed? It doesn't matter if you live to be a thousand years old if you just live the same day over and over again.

(Q.: How do you get the energy on and how do you keep it on?) Well, the last time I was faced with that problem was when I came back from the Guatemala and Vancouver tours and I didn't have any, and had to go about getting it on. I had to retreat a little bit because I had run it down pretty extremely; but then I started going about getting it on, up to a point that meant collecting myself and understanding myself and having a little time for my mind to digest the events that had gone on, so I didn't have an overload of things that were so heavy that they needed pondering that I'd been too busy to ponder—let go of that kind of stuff and try to eat good and try to catch up on sleep. And then there came a point where everything was all right, except that I just didn't have any appetite. I heard something said by one of the kids in the house that keeps horses, "You can't just eat if you don't do anything; you have to go *do something.*" Well, my family doesn't like to let me out of the house with an empty stomach, and I had to say, "No, you got to let me go with an empty stomach; when I come back I'll be hungry, I promise." And I went out and I started to do things that I hadn't been able to do for a while, of taking care of business and doing stuff, and it was two o'clock in the afternoon before I noticed that I hadn't had breakfast, and I went home and ate a lot. And all my energy systems started coming on. And when I was first breaking over halfway, starting to gain was when I said, "Well, today I have my energy starting to come on," and I caught a cold the same day, and the cold didn't make any difference. I just went right on through gaining energy and getting stronger and being able to do more, at the same time going through the change of a little sniffle in the nose and a little sore throat and those changes; but I was already over the hump and it didn't make any difference. That's the thing about if you catch a lot of bugs or something—you have to get up over the other side of the energy hump. If you ride on the right place on the energy hump you don't get so many bugs because you're stronger, you just truck right on through them.

You're an organism, and at a biological level it's you and them, and one of you is going to inherit that piece of protoplasm. With somebody who's had a baby or somebody who's had a heavy thing happen to them, there comes a point frequently when you have to go to them and say, "Now get up and truck. Start accumulating some juice." Well, we've been laying back here all winter saying, "What can we do? What can we do? We can't do much," but now we can do something and it's coming into time to do something and we're ready to do something, and we're actually pretty strong. We are fat and good-looking for having survived the worst winter in a hundred and nine years at what some people describe as the edge of poverty. Just look at these folks. My father called up and wanted to know how we survived the winter and stuff. Better than the folks that were dependent on natural gas.

But the thing about getting your energy on is that you can't have any little leaks. It's like a system that you're trying to fill.

The air system on the Greyhound is supposed to run 120 pounds at least, and sometimes it has enough leaks in it that with the compressor working as hard as it can, it can only maintain something like 100 pounds. And you drive it with 100 pounds, but you would rather like to know that the whole system was tight—and it's all a continuing thing, because it's an old bus and we have to go over it and tighten it again and again and again. That's how everybody is, that's how your mind is: you have to go out and tighten it again and again and again. You can get sloppy about stuff; I have to watch myself year by year that I don't get sloppy of mouth. I don't mind talking down-home and beatnik and possibly even faintly dirty by some folks' calculations of it, because I want to speak the language that I've spoken all my life because it will convey what I want to say the most. But at the same time I don't want to get so much into badmouth that I detract in too many folks' minds from the spiritual beauty and majesty of reality, of the Lotus. So I have to go and check myself out and every so often I hear myself saying to myself, "That's a little loose, watch your mouth."

I know somebody who's into the juice and who says really horrible things to you—conceptually horrible: they don't have much juice and they don't get said very loud and there's not very much energy behind them and they're not very truthful and they don't have very much likelihood of being true, and therefore, are pretty harmless, except for their emotional content, which is picking on your innermost thing—being overweight, something that would bug you that he tries to get into you about. And he lays out this stuff with very low energy delivery, just vavavava, terrible sounding vavavava. Well, the thing is, it doesn't cost much to manufacture that terrible sounding stuff, and if you don't put much into the delivery, it doesn't cost you much to publish it, but if you're around anybody who is torn up by the idea that they think their teenage acne hasn't cleared up soon enough, who is going to be hit by a personal attack at that level, he doesn't have to say it very loud. If it's going to work at all, all he has to do is imply it, to take somebody off their energy and take their energy. And that's like fishing for the energy: "Anybody going to bite over there?" And when he finds somebody who bites, he just engages him into a ball of knots in a very short time, until he runs their energy down enough that they aren't interesting anymore and then he'll move on to a juicier pasture. I've found several folks like that.

If you find yourself engaged in one of those, you can't have any feathers that can be plucked, or they will be plucked; and you can't care, because if you care you are not any help, you are just another source of energy to be plucked.

Be nice to each other. Dig the old formalities that try to make it so people who don't know each other share the energy. Shaking hands is nothing but being tantric with someone, to say, "I'm going to be straight enough with you that we can join hands, and that we can let our energy flow back and forth along that channel, we'll share energy at that level; and then we'll go ahead and discuss what business we have to discuss, but we've shared life force and shared energy and affirmed our essential Oneness through that tantric connection." It's an age-old thing to hold on to somebody and feel that, to embrace somebody. When you send the kids to bed the reason you take them and embrace them and kiss them before you send them to bed is to charge them with a lot of juice, pump 'em up, send them off to bed with a lot of energy on so they'll have a good peaceful night. All these old social customs and things are ways to help stir a lot of people's energy back and forth. There are some people that are juicier than some people; run them all around together so everybody exchanges vibes, and stir it around a little bit, give everybody a good chance at it. Everybody looks red-cheeked and happy after a good "Turkey in the Straw" stomp.

When I'm home, sometimes I try to get some rest just for the sake of letting all my vibes settle. But when I'm on the road I can't afford to be any way other than a very open position, and I let anybody say anything they want to me, pretty much, just so I can listen to what happens to me when I hear it. And if there's any place where it makes me go "Oops," like that, then I have to go and figure out that place, so it doesn't make me do that, so that I can be invulnerable—so I can be invisible on those wave lengths. Anyone should be able to say anything they want to you and it shouldn't bug you. If it ain't true, it ain't true; if it's true, it's true. If it's unkind and ill-thought about, you know that, and you allow for it. If there's anybody whose sudden presence puts you uptight, if there's any subject that makes you uptight to hear about it, you're not free; you can be moved around to do anything if you have enough handles like that sticking out.

There is a question in spiritual teachings of, How do you keep your head when all about you are losing theirs? How do you keep your head under attack? How do you keep your head when somebody is either mad or angry, or just trying to rip you off, or taking advantage of the situation or just trying to condition you? How can you defend yourself, how can you walk through that? Now we all know the characteristics of somebody who can really do that. Mahatma Gandhi walked through religious blood feuds in India, riots and open warfare in the streets. And he walked through the streets at about ninety-three pounds in his dao-dao, and not only did they not harm him, but the riots quit around him wherever he went. And he truly did not care for the Hindus over the Moslems or the Moslems over the Hindus or the right-wingers over the left-wingers or the left-wingers over the right-wingers; *he truly wanted peace for the people, for all the people, and no one that was sane would touch him, and the man who got him was a poor, misguided, misled thing.*

When you're under attack, your energy goes through a certain exchange. The best way to do something is to know where it's at well enough that you're almost transparent to it. I had the privilege of having a place like that at our Vancouver gig, because there were some folks that I almost knew were going to be into the juice. They were into the juice already, and I knew that when we reached the concentrations of energy that we could get up to, that they were going to be into the juice. And sure enough, it was the kind of gig that when I stepped off the stage there were about three people trying to take the microphone away from me—wanting to do anything from announce a lost dog to "Let me sing one now," and this one couple was pretty out of it. He was screaming and hollering and she was doing this thing—she came over to me and she stood right in front of me and she had long fingernails and she poked me in the belly button repeatedly with her long fingernails and screamed at me and hollered at me; and she screamed so loud and so harshly at me that I could tell from the tone of the scream that she could only do it two or three more times— she was not going to be able to do that for very long. So I just waited and relaxed and listened to her throat deteriorate over the next two or three screams until she had to quit because she couldn't bear to do it anymore, and she used up all her juice, and she put out her whole thing and I stood very quiet and very still so the crowd didn't jump and didn't get uptight, and a nice lady from the audience took charge of the girl and the energy stayed just like it was, and *we stayed essentially transparent to that.* But that's because you know that there's nothing in that situation threatening, that everybody could understand that here's a girl who's just blown out by the energy; everybody really understands that kind of thing. Just popping out of the subconscious.

Public school teachers in regular square schools, if they see a kid behaving dangerously at an intersection, are required by law to take that child in hand—even if it's not a child from their school and they are not in the school district where they work and it's out of school hours, just because it's somebody that does it with a bunch of kids. They are the on-duty grownup on the spot. They have a legal obligation to do that. And that's what it is here—not like a legal obligation but a moral obligation. For you to take care of *us.* Whenever something happens to *us* I say, "Who is taking care of *us?*" I want to know who is taking care of *us.*

(Q.: Do you think that whales are any smarter for heading back to the ocean?) I'll tell you, the whale's brain is larger than a man's and more complicated. And the interesting thing about this is, if you take a porpoise and a shark of equal size, the shark's brain will be about the size of your thumb, and the porpoise's brain will be larger than a human's. And the shark and the porpoise swim equally well; a shark can do everything it needs to survive—have its young, do its trip, reproduce, swim around, respond to stimuli, its eyeballs work, all of its systems work and all that stuff—off a little brain about the size of your thumb and here's this porpoise with a brain bigger than a human's. *What does he do with the rest of his head?*

The stories they tell about the whales and the porpoises showing intelligence are uncanny, and we just have to respond to that intelligence when we can. At the same time, you have to respond to that intelligence in your spouse.

This is a nice stoned place; we came out of that into a nice stoned place, almost as stoned as the one we brought out of the meditation. Feel the energy. Very stoned Holy Spirit, healing. It helps make us One, helps make us closer to God. It helps make us understand other people's religion and helps make ours more understandable to other people. It is a manifestation of Holy Spirit, that's communion. I think this is a very stoned place and if it's all right with you, I don't want to do any more nuts-and-bolts from here, this feels like such a good place to take home. I just love you all so much and I thank you so much for helping in this. All of us together are going to make a great big difference that is going to help out mankind and God for a long time. I love you. Good morning.

February 13, 1977

Ringing Bells and Burning Incense

This morning in the meditation, I just felt long rushes of great shuddering sighs of letting it off and of letting go of heart because I think all of us had a knock on our heart to have a fire on the Farm and to have someone get really seriously injured and not survive it. We had a knock on all of our hearts and I felt in the meditation it was like we were together and shared that among us as much as we could. There's a thing that Barbara said when she first looked at Emma after Emma died. She said, "I somehow feel like I failed her or something." I told her she didn't and that she was a good mother and that she got burned in the same fire, trying to do her best. But she had that feeling in her heart and the thing about that feeling in her heart was—it wasn't that there wasn't a feeling like that, it just didn't belong any more to her heart than it did to the whole grown-up world, because somewhere in there the grown-up world wasn't quite safe enough for that tender thing. So it's a knock on all of our hearts and we all know that. On the way to meditation this morning I was like a long-distance runner making that last few yards to the tape. I was just really glad I had a while to sit before I had to do anything. And the way we have to be about that is just like I said earlier to the couple I just married, "For better or for worse." And that's how we take each other, the whole Farm family takes each other for better or for worse. And if it's worse we share it all, and it makes it easier to share it that way.

Sometimes when people watch the news on the television and they watch somebody catching a real hard time somewhere else they say, "Wow, sure glad it ain't happening here." But it *is* happening here; because we aren't separate from the folks who it's happening to. And it's just like that when we lose a kid, there's no glad-it-wasn't-one-of-my-kids, because they're all my kids, and they're all our kids. That's part of the agreement that we make. Not in some kind of strange communal raising of the kids in a herd and not telling them who their folks are kind of conceptual thing, but just that *we make it safe for all the kids.*

Vulnerable. That's a word that came to me in meditation this morning. Vulnerable. You know what the trip is with the way we run the Farm? It's not just that we're immensely huge and immensely strong, because we are. It's that we run our business in such a way that we're vulnerable. Business-like people don't run their businesses so they're vulnerable. They do it like playing chess. If they move a piece they look and see if anything else has command of that place they're about to occupy. You don't move onto a place where you're going to get snapped up on the next move. You can't be vulnerable and play chess; the game won't last very long. That's the thing that we do, is we be vulnerable. That's why we had that kind of fire in the first place.

We're getting so big. When we had only a couple of hundred people, you could get to where you knew where everyone was at, down to the minute. It's kind of hard to do that with something this big. But we need to be this big because we aren't functional if we're not this big. A few weeks ago when a lot of people were off the Farm, we felt skinny. We couldn't do our thing, there wasn't enough of us, we weren't really functional.

The way we are right now is, we're so big that to understand the situation on any given day is almost impossible: we have so many other variables that string down through time that we almost can't cut a thin enough slice for us to have a Gestalt understanding of the whole thing. Everybody hip to that? It seems that what we have to do is to go in the direction of hotting up our communication about stuff until we have more of a chance of cutting that slice and seeing what the given situation is at any time. We don't have up-to-the-minute information as tight as we need to. This is talking about getting us smarter.

The equation that Bucky uses about wealth: Some people think the stuff is the wealth. He says that the stuff *times the knowledge* is the wealth. Well, we're working on wealth the hard way, by the hour. Now as far as knowledge is concerned, we ought to smart up; and we can multiply wealth that way.

In a group head, smarting up is about communication between people. Now this is a funny kind of school. Part of it is an assumption—not so much that there's a body of knowledge, because there's no body of knowledge other than what is self-evident to all sane observers—but *there is some level of consciousness that will allow you to see.* There is an assumption of ground rules.

What Etta from Guatemala said is, "If I got something in me and I don't say it, it makes me stink." The assumption that we're working behind is that we're going to be communicative enough with each other to discuss things. What I find happening sometimes is that people don't say anything until what they say is in the nature of a complaint. If you lay back and don't say anything until what you have to say is a complaint, the question is, "Why weren't you trying to do something about it before?"

Vanderbilt Hospital has some very good departments. Their intensive care for premature infants is one of the most impressive things I've ever seen for really a high-level spiritual medical trip. And there are other good departments. But it's so big that you can go from one department to another and they lose pieces of knowledge about you in the transfer—someone who saw you commits what they saw to a paper and the piece of paper goes with you to somebody else and the next person doesn't look at you, they read the piece of paper. A certain attention to detail is lost. We send a fair amount of people to the hospital along with the patient: we always detail a couple of people to go along and go to the hospital with them to protect them from the hospital—in order that they may get a fair shake, from having to deal with that machine, the individual parts of which are people, and normal bell curve of distribution—some of them real fine, some of them pretty sleazy, and a bunch of them trying in the middle there.

The reason that I tell you all this is so you can see something that's establishment. Now I have trouble being identified with the establishment myself. But there's a way where the Farm is an establishment, because an establishment is something that's established, and we've been here a while: we're the oldest permanent floating crap game in town. In getting our thing done from the clinic to the housing department to the Gate to the visitors' tent from one place to another, we have a tendency to lose people in the cracks a little, just like Vanderbilt. This is about the Farm being smart. Every time anybody gets caught in one of those cracks and gets mishandled, they assume, unless they can get to know better, that that's the Farm policy—because that's what happened to *them*. The only way to get to know what the policy is, is by what happens to you. The policy ain't anything conceptual; the policy is what happens to you.

This is Part II—Theory and Practice. Now I had a letter from a lady the other day who ...id, "You know, I was never revolutionary before. I was attracted to you by qualities of love and truth, and when I came to the Farm you sparked me on to being revolutionary, but I forget about it sometimes and it doesn't seem . . ." Then she says that she wants to understand it more, how come I'm that way. *The way I got revolutionary is by following love and truth. And by following love and truth you see that if you know what's going on and you can do something, then you have to.* We're pacifists, and we realize that we're not just pacifists physically about fists and sticks and guns, but that we're pacifists psychologically—we don't intimidate, scare, browbeat or back each other off.

Once again I find myself wanting to say, "Don't think that we don't have a path if it isn't drawn on like the white line on the highway." I think, "Why should I be in a position of saying that after all these years?" *What we are doing here is a path.* Pay attention, because if you don't understand it as a path and if you aren't trying to tread that path, you are left out of the major information circuits on the Farm, because that's the one that everyone's in on. That's the thing you ought to know to understand why you are doing this. I hate to see anybody leave the Farm unhappy about it, because I feel like if you understand what's going on, you shouldn't be unhappy about it, you should be proud to be part of it, and privileged. So much of our path breaks down to such simple stuff like the Zen aphorism—*If you don't know what to do in the morning, get up and make the bed and eat breakfast and wash the dishes and clean the house.* If you still don't know what to do, go back to work and continue—until you get straight or it kills you. Ain't that right? We don't really die. We're just like a quarterback caught with the last gun going off before he can throw the last pass into the end zone. He didn't lose; he just wasn't done. Ran out of time, man. You don't lose, you just run out of time.

That's supposed to be spiritual, the stuff I said. It's supposed to exalt you. It's supposed to exalt you like I was ringing bells and burning incense.

The way this path is supposed to be is nonconceptual—you live life how it really has to be lived. We all mourn for Emma, not because we want to but because it is what we have at this time as the result of our karma. We have *to mourn,* that's what we have for a while, for a reasonable time. Dr. Williams told me one time, "Almost every time I ever lose a patient, I deliver a baby within twenty-four hours." Now he's had a lot of patients and he's lost a lot of them, and he is open and vulnerable to that, and he mourns and grieves when he loses one, but he has to go on—which is how we all are. I'll tell you what, I'll take a question.

138

(Question.) Well, just like the rest of the society, the very language of our thing gets devalued until we say, "Wow, it was really stoned," when it *wasn't* really stoned, it was just acceptable; and they say, "It was really psychedelic," when they mean that we came to enough of an agreement not to part enemies. That devalues our trip, and we ain't *tripping* like we used to. We could stand a fair amount of abuse of that kind when we were getting our mind blown once a week. Now we're older and we have longer-range plans than to be able to afford to blow our minds once a week. We have to remember something from one week to the next.

I want to teach you about how to make it through not making the neighbors mad and getting past with the bills good and doing that kind of stuff, because I really think that will create the sane and stable society in which we can really spiritually flower; and at the same time I don't want to be just at the pitchfork end of it all the time. The teaching that came to me is that *you get high when you get high,* and if you don't pay attention you may have missed it, and you don't know when your next one is coming. I try to bring about a high every Sunday, and every time I gig I try to bring it to a communion. There have only been a few times when I felt I didn't make it to a communion.

I think as the Farm has more and more people that didn't come on the Caravan, it has thinned out the information from Monday Night Class about being into the juice.

There are all kinds of very subtle ways that people can be into the juice. And here's the thing about a subtle way of being into the juice and a gross way of being into the juice: It doesn't make any difference as to *how much juice it gets.* In fact, that's the nature of the game. If you can do something like jump up and scream, "AAAHHHHHH!" and try to get the juice, a bunch of folks will sock it to you—a high level of attention focused and directed pretty hard, so you get a certain amount of juice. If the Pope, while speaking to a group of people, were to use the wrong number of fingers in a benediction, it would blow minds harder than some longhair getting up and screaming; it would cause the same thing. There can be a massive transfer of juice for a very subtle cause. Now somebody that's a good rip-off knows how to give the least energy in the trigger or the cause that sets it off, in order to reap the biggest benefit of energy after they subtract their initial investment. I've seen kids that had it down so cold that they could drive both parents completely up the wall by clearing their throat in a certain way. *"Stop that.* Close your mouth. Breathe through your nose. Quit that!"

Or you tell a kid, "Quit crying. Now stop that crying."

"WWAAA."

"Stop that crying."

And they go, "All right. (sniffle.)"

"Come on, don't do that."

They say, "Okay. (sniffle.)"

Well, then a kid has you to where they can just do little things to you and let you do all the big reactions, and all they have to do is grunt. Or take a little kid that has a nice smile, so a lot of people come up and say, "Hi," and flash one on him so he'll flash one back to them, so after a while he gets to where all he has to do is just wiggle the corner of his mouth like Elvis Presley, and his mother says, "Oohhh." That's where Elvis Presley was at; all he had to do was just stand there and just wiggle his lip and they'd fall out for rows and rows and rows.

I believe that there are basically two kinds of human behavior: sane, self-directed, self-actualized on purpose; and the other one is into the juice. Because everybody's subconscious will be into the juice—none of us can say that our subconscious is so clean that we never take a swipe at the juice; everybody I know gets into the juice. I have to watch it, because I expect to be high, I think I ought to be reasonably high all the time, so if I'm not I'm out there finding out how come. When you talk about the formality of church, the reason that like most churches are so very formal is that everybody had to sit in a row and a pew and say the same thing in unison together to try to make them straighten up enough to not be into the juice to create a communion. And we don't have to be quite that formal in a way, we don't sit in rows and don't have to say the *Prajna Paramita Sutra* every time—we might talk about it, ask questions about it; everything is *Prajna Paramita Sutra.*

But just being a little crossways is into the juice. Sometimes people play with the energy—it's like tennis. Imagine if you bat the ball to the other person and it goes over to the other side and the net suddenly got ten feet tall, and the ball didn't come back. Well, that's what happens when you're going along and you say, "Hi Sam, hi Joe, what's happening?" And then you say hello to somebody and they go "Myah."

"How's things?"

"Pretty good, I guess."

"How's everything? What say?"

"Aah, pretty good."

That ain't what you put out when someone says, "Hey, how are you?" That's being into the juice. All those are unfair energy exchanges.

A lot of people be like a short-change artist. Short-change artists that work in restaurants will just take about fifteen cents off of every transaction, and they can just about mess you up enough that you can miss down to about fifteen cents, and it's only fifteen cents, three hundred customers a day. And there are folks like that, even here on the Farm, who every time you deal with them, somewhere in there—you know, they just make their voice be enough not true when they say, "Everything's fine," that it takes about fifteen cents off your transaction because it isn't bad enough necessarily for you to go back and say, "Oh yeah? What's wrong?" but it's just enough for you to have to say, "Oh, that wasn't quite right," and you go around with a little hook hanging in your head. That's being into the juice.

Some folks have a level to which they can be honest about the energy, but if it goes beyond that level they're not cleared, there's like a security clearance or something, and they're not cleared for the next level of energy. The only thing you can do is to try to educate someone and show them their subconscious, because nobody in their right mind would do that, if they were working with their conscious mind. The thing that really proves it is that you see people do things for energy at times and at places that you could not understand, unless you knew that it was for that incredible precious energy: they will get into a birthing, they will get into a funeral, they will get into anything if they're blown out above the level where they are able to handle the juice.

Well, keeping from being paranoid is like taking a bath often enough. Blowing out from high energy levels like that is from not taking enough responsibility about what you're supposed to be doing in life, on the Farm and everywhere, and if you think, "Well, the heavyweights are going to take care of the heavy stuff and I'm not going to bother to be heavy because nobody's ever going to try me out because I'm safely in the shadow of these heavyweights who are taking the brunt of it," one of these days you're going to wander into the sun and melt. You're going to find yourself deeply, blatantly, in front of everybody, into the juice and embarrassed as hell about it. I think the main thing about understanding about being into the juice is that *you have to get high enough to experience some juice yourself.* Energy is just like that old television station out there. If you get your television fixed, *you will get the picture.*

Anything anybody thinks we ought to do here? I feel well connected to you, I just love you a bunch. If there's anything you need to say, . . . Three or four years ago, I said, "You know what? We're going to become controversial," and we *are* controversial; and all that it's really necessary to do about that is to continue to cook. If we continue to cook it's all right if we're a little controversial now, just so we keep cooking.

I'm not one of those determinists that say that the people who got killed in the war had it coming from bad karma—I think that's some kind of bullshit, is what that is. I tried to think of a better term but that's the best I could do with it. But I do believe that the *people always outnumber the government, and the kind of government you have is the kind of government that you deserve, because it's the kind of govern-*

ment that you have let happen. On the Farm in Lewis County in Tennessee in the United States, the government that we have is the one we have built and let happen and created. And folks that don't speak up deserve what they get; and that's different than saying that those folks that get wasted in wars had it coming. That's not what I'm saying. There's some places where you can't speak up—it's too deadly. Speaking up is non-survival for some folks, and that means that some other folks that are *not* under that gun, . . . I can say here in Tennessee that *the people who are shooting priests down in South America are cowards.* I can say that from here because I'm not right in front of that gun, and hope that it goes out from here. We must speak up for all those folks that cannot, because the world is one world, and if we don't speak up, . . .

I want everyone to feel real clear about what we're doing and why we're doing it. We're not just doing it for ourselves. If we're just doing it for ourselves, I'd rather move to Cleveland and change my name. But at the same time, doing it for everybody else means that we have to be sure that all us folks are healthy and fed, because if we aren't starting from healthy and fed and safe here, then we aren't sending out a safe signal to the folks on this planet; and there is a lot of dumb information going around on this planet already—there are ideas of karma that are so medieval, that it's a shame that people are being sucked in by them. But I think that more and more you are going to find that people are going to require that somebody that calls himself spiritual do it for someone besides himself.

I guess what I'm saying is sort of a statement about hinayana and mahayana. Here's the thing you ought to learn about being heroes of the revolution. Nobody that has it knocked gets to be a hero. You understand that? If you have it made, you don't get to be a hero; if you want to have it made, you won't be a hero. You want to be Mighty Mouse and streak across the sky with your red cape leaving a trail when you come down to get the cat out of the mice's business.

I guess I'll let you go. I could rap on you for days. I just wanted to let you know that I was interested in your case. Good morning. I love you.

February 6, 1977

There Is No Farm

This is our first meeting in three weeks, and I started off this morning thinking, "Let's get down to business," first thing; and then, as usual, an hour of meditation takes the edge off that. The main thing I feel when I get here is that I love you so much. Just trying, wanting us to do good. And it's that time of year that we have to stop thinking about survival as a goal, and start thinking about dazzling everybody with our fancy footwork, which is another order of magnitude. I got interviewed this week by a nice lady who is going to do a story on us. She kept asking me what I did, and I kept telling her stuff I did and stuff I did; and realized that none of the stuff I told her I did was really the stuff I did. She asked good questions, pushing me back up, saying, "What do you do? What do you do?" and finally I had to say, "Well, what I *really* do is know that God is real from my own personal experience, and be sane and reasonably accessible, containing that knowledge; that's what I basically do, and then anything else I have time for to help out, of course—anything I can do. But basically it comes down to really knowing that we are all One and knowing that God is real. And I understand why we're doing this." I think a lot of you understand why we're doing this better when we're doing it better, and when we're just surviving through the winter I think you tend to forget what it is we are doing.

One of the things in our consciousness that I have to struggle against the hardest is the idea that the Farm is some kind of abstract entity that exists apart from us, because the idea that the Farm exists apart from us in any way makes it possible for any one of us to forget what it is that we do willingly for each other here—not what the Farm does for us, but what we do willingly for each other; and the Farm has no existence apart from that. And that was easier to remember, in a way, when we first arrived in school buses and we went through our first winter when you had about an eighteen-inch-high toy stove in a school bus and you could fire it up until it was red-hot all over and sit within two feet of it and it wouldn't do anything. This isn't the first winter we had; we had twelve below zero at the barn the second winter we were here. But the majority of the folks did not come here on the Caravan. We've been through some other things since then, we've been busted; we had the Hundred Cases of Contaminated Watercress Hepatitis Summer, and the Wheatberry Winter and now the Winter of '77.

I've heard this one particular attitude lately, which is that "I can't get the Farm to back my project. I have a project going and I can't get the Farm to back my project." *There is no Farm to back your project.* We are not separated into funders-of-projects and doers-of-projects, we are just trying to keep on keeping on, to make a difference for a lot of other people besides us. We are the fattest first-hand beneficiaries of this agreement; but there are a lot of people all over the country that are really given a great deal of hope by our continued existence.

How do we continue to exist? Doing this thing has been declared impossible by a certain sociologist of our acquaintance; but like the bumble bee, we are not interested in our possibility, only our probability. Now there is nothing to take care of you apart from us. Everything that happens is done by somebody.

We're coming into Springtime, and a whole lot of what happens on the Farm is sort of like setting out onions—they get bigger and you harvest them, but you have to set out every one of them individually; and it doesn't sprout, grow vines, multiply, or do anything: it's just that the ones you put in the ground get bigger, and you dig them up someday. A lot of stuff on the Farm you just work at and work at, and it gets bigger. Somebody's got to do it; somebody has to say, "I'll take responsibility for this."

Now when somebody wants a project funded or backed up, they say, "Well, maybe there is some free money, maybe I should go out and get a job to fund my project." Well good, that's a good way to do it, but you shouldn't fool yourself that any job within distance of the Farm hasn't already been accounted for in the budget by the Board, clear out to Nashville, clear down to Alabama. Any job that you can find anywhere in this area has already been accounted for by the Board of Directors, and they are expecting that; how about that? We are a giant creature here in a pretty thinly distributed ecology— there ain't very many rabbits around here for a bear this size.

A certain number of us can grow enough food on this soil to exist at a survival level, but as far as *doing anything* goes, we have to do a thing so much bigger than this. I want the Farm to think bigger. Do the work in the square-inch field, but don't just restrict your consciousness to the square-inch field. I find a lot of folks who have their consciousness restricted to their square-inch field until they're unhappy and don't know what they are doing anymore. *You've got to know why we are doing this: we are doing this because this seems to be the only sane alternative to a completely insane society.*

The Board decided lately that we couldn't afford a computer right now. Well, that's reasonable: we can't. On the other hand, you can program me—I ain't doing anything else. But we do have a computer at our disposal, we do, and it's T.V. Let me tell you what I saw happen, and see if you saw this, too.

A few weeks ago some dude took a hostage, and he got national T.V. off of it. About a week later, another cat takes a hostage, and he's all prepared—he doesn't even have to hold the gun on him, he has the gun wired to him, so he just walks down and holds it like the end of a leash; and he does this for a while, and they promise him that they are going to lay off him if he gives up. And then he gives up, and they break all the promises and lock him up. Everybody pretty much knew it. Then they interview the man who made the decision to get him back, and he said that he'd have promised *anything* to get the hostages back, and he discussed his reasoning and how he'd do it—and all this comes out, nationally televised.

Then another man gets a hostage. And he says he's not going to sell out easy like the other one—because he watched it and he's learning from the computer—the computer is teaching these people. So this one, he gets to talk to the President: the President says that he'll come and talk to him if he lets the hostages go; so he did, and sure enough Jimmy talks to him. They lock him up anyhow, but Jimmy talks to him. So we've had our lesson in hostages from the computer.

And the next lesson we get is Idi Amin, who takes 200-some Americans and won't let them out of the country, and he's holding hostages; but he has hostages too, and it becomes very plain that if he jumps off on those Americans, Jimmy is going to jump off on *him*—and he understands that he has a whole country, so he has hostages too; and his ratio isn't so good, because he's betting his whole country against just two or three hundred.

And then you get a dude in D.C. and he has the main B'nai B'rith headquarters in D.C. with a hundred people on the top floor, and an Islamic mosque and a district Federal building— about a hundred and twenty people in three different buildings: and with about a dozen people invested, he has about half as many hostages as Idi Amin, and he only has twelve troops invested. And then he talks over the telephone to the T.V.; he says, "You ain't going to promise anything and break your promise like you did with that other dude," having learned from the computer—and Jimmy Carter broke the ice by getting into the last one. Well, Jimmy did good; he invited three heavy Moslem ambassadors, and they all went in there with the *Koran* and said things like, "The Prophet spoke of mercy," or something along that line, and he had to cop, and it was so intelligent of Jimmy to run it as a religious question and send in religious folks instead of troops.

But the leader of the trip, who has taken a hundred people hostage, one person killed and lots of people hurt—a bunch of folks got their faces kicked in—is out on his own recognizance, no bail, because *that was his price;* they had to negotiate with him and they had to keep it. And by this time even the heat is beginning to learn from the computer, and the one that made that decision said something like, "If we don't keep the faith with them, they won't keep the faith with us in the future and we won't have any basis to negotiate from if we ever have that situation again. We're going to have to keep the faith with what we say, like it or not." There is this computer, and it teaches. I don't know if the T.V. has figured out that they almost got a hundred people wasted.

If anybody making any of those decisions, from network decisions to police decisions right down the line, had checked with anybody that had been around here for a while they'd say, "Oh! The more juice you put into it, the more you're going to get." Now we have some ideas about what kind of juice is good juice to put out. We want to be *recognized as something*— we don't want to be so bizarre that nobody can identify with us.

There is a whole thing back out in there that we are not separate from. We can't cloister up. Now the thing that happened with that hostage trip was a *random teaching* from the computer. It was random; they did not want the result; it took them a few weeks to discover the result that they were getting, even. The seeds of action sown in the fields of causality.

Another phrase I've heard from a couple of people is "accomplishing anything"—some of you who have been here for a while don't feel like you've accomplished anything. It depends on what you identify with, I suppose, whether you've accomplished anything or not—or whether you even think that we are we, I guess, makes a difference whether you think that *we've* accomplished anything or not.

149

And when I talk to you in this field, I get stuff back. I got a letter from a gentleman up in Vancouver, British Columbia, who says the Farm seems pretty nice but you talk about all these husbands intimidating their wives and it makes me kind of scared, and I don't know if I want to . . . where's the Farm at if that's where it's at, or what's all that going on? I get kickback from Canada for having spoken of that. We are not a place where a lot of intimidation goes on of the ladies by the husbands or the husbands by the ladies—we are virtually one of the only places in the world where anyone mentions it or does anything about it, or where it is even worthy of being brought up; and that's why it makes that sound here because we talk about it, and that's always the thing that I bring out here on Sunday morning: Should I say the thing? This morning I could have come out and not even have meditated. I could have just come out and said, "All right, let's get down to business," but I thought, "No, I should sit down and meditate. We're soggy because we ain't met for a few weeks." But I thought we were supposed to be trippers—thunder yogis. I thought we're supposed to be somewhat heroic, even if it's corny. I believe that was the agreement, even if it's corny.

To renew our agreements—I'll tell you what I found out while I was deep stoned—I got a letter from a dude who says, "Where did you get your early groundwork about energetics?" He's getting it from working in a mental hospital, and he's looking at the ward like a black box, and then going inside the black box and trying to figure out the circuits of what makes it so weird, figuring out the wires.

We are trippers, and we consider that some of us are just out-front trippers, and some of us have tripped other ways. We were trippers. We came here in seven months on caravan in school buses on the road, and slept in rest stops on the freeway at night, and the semi's go by all night long, and we got rousted by the cops an average of better than once a day. We'd get rousted every time we tried to stop for the night, and every time we crossed a state line.

There is the question of, "What does being together and working together mean?" Are we going to do what it is that we need done? We have a lot of stuff that we need done. I've had a couple or three folks come to me and say they thought they had to go somewhere else to get to *do something,* to get to get out. We have some folks that say they want to get out and they can't get out, when it's obvious that we are not covered, we are in an uncovered and vulnerable situation as we now stand—they can hear that in Vancouver, too—we are the most successful one of these in the world, and we are wide open and vulnerable—as they say in chess, *gardé.* Also, some people

talk to me like they don't know what their commitment is. I think that if you don't know what your commitment is, you almost have an obligation to be gone by sundown. I told somebody else,

"I don't know what *you're* going to do, but I'm going to stay here and accept the bills as they come in." And that is where the vast majority of the Farm is at.

I bought three magnets for fifteen cents apiece—the round magnets with a hole in the middle, and you can slide them over a pencil and they'll float—so I got these three magnets and I thought, "A magnet for each of the kids," and then I thought the three of them could get together and they'd have three magnets, enough to do some stuff with. But the first thing that happened was each kid took his own magnet and ran away with it and ran around with it clutched in his hand. It might as well be a rock. So then I took a tray and I started to make them go around, and as soon as they moved one of the kids would go, "Ah-ha!" and snatch it. That went on for a minute, and then one of them started catching on. I said, "Okay, now put your hand underneath and move it around, try to move it over and catch the other magnets." So he's catching on and just fixing to do it, except he can't concentrate because the other one is right on his back going, "Let-me-do-it-let-me-do-it, can-I-do-it-now," etc., and I'm trying to turn them on to the principles of magnetism and stuff, as fast as I can—I see that I should have gotten two magnets each for a start.

And I feel like the Board of Directors is like the kids with the magnets, and some of the other independent operators are like the kid that's standing behind, saying let-me-try-it-let-me-try-it. But that's a funny way to look at it, because from the viewpoint that me and the Board have, it's finding enough reliable people that will still be there tomorrow and still be your friend and still be doing the project and won't trip out to some other state or take off in the middle of a project or bug out on you—to find enough reliable people to try to accomplish something in an adult fashion. I would like to use a lot of these folks around here who have a lot of technical abilities and educations and skills and stuff, but some of those folks are some of the most unusable people we have, *because they won't make their thing available to anybody.* They act like they bought that knowledge in college and if they don't get their $20,000 a year out of it they were burnt.

I know a lot of people I can name, who weren't responsible at a point, and decided that they'd be responsible at a point. One of them was holding down a pretty important job and he got sick and had to have an operation, and he said he was going to quit doing all that thing—and he was the only one that knew about it. So we had this long talk about it,

"Are you going to walk out in the middle of it? You're the only one that knows that thing, are you going to bug out in the middle of it?"

And he says, "Okay, I'll stay until it gets covered."

Well, that was some years ago and he's still doing it, the same thing, and it's a good thing, too—we ain't got anybody else to cover it yet.

Now there are some folks that have no responsibility at all—a certain number of kids might as well be living in New York City for all they care about what's going on; and that's a shame, because those kids aren't being reached, because they aren't realizing why we are doing this. They don't understand some of the things that the Gate crew has had to face, just to make it so this could be a place where a kid could walk around by himself. This can't just be the kind of a place where the same few folks work themselves to death all the time until they collapse, and another few folks, almost equally predictable, gripe.

We are interdependent, mutually responsible; what one of you does affects another one; one of you dragging your feet means another one has to do the work.

When I was sick I read this science fiction book about magicians. It was a place where, when a rain cloud came across that country it went in a zig-zag pattern from all the different magicians wishing it on to their farm or off of this town or onto that farm—it zig-zagged across the country and it had to go out to sea to be allowed to rain in peace without everyone having so much opinions about where it went. They were heavy into their lick. And they did a lot of good magic. There is a place in the book where the dude is sailing into the wind, almost dead into the wind, he's really taking an extreme tack, and they're just beating hard upwind in a small open boat into the ocean. And his apprentice has seen him up and do heavy magic stuff, and says, "Well, man, how come you don't up and throw a little wind into the sail? Let's get this show on the road, come on with some magic, get the wind going and get on through here so we don't have to fight this." And he says, "I would not add a stone to someone that is already sore burdened."

And when you think in terms of, "Let the Farm do it," think in terms of how big a stone are you willing to lay on somebody that is already working pretty hard—or could you carry it yourself, because you-carrying-it-yourself is still the Farm carrying it; if you do it, that's the Farm doing it. A lot of people think that the Farm doing it means somebody besides them, for them instead of them. Somebody wants the Board of Directors to give them money for a project when the money is coming in from pounding nails. Why put in the middle man? Why don't you just go out and pound the nails, instead?

One of the hardest things for me to do on Sunday morning is to name names. It's not that I don't name names all the time as a policy—sometimes I think maybe I ought to. I used to at certain times—when we had sort of extreme Haight Street level of rip-offs among us, I used to not be shy about naming them, so that folks would know, you know? We're overall so much saner than we used to be that we don't hardly ever have that level of heavy magic rip-off thing happening, do we? Or if it's happening in your house and you ain't talking about it, how come? Ain't it a lot saner, notwithstanding everything? Can anybody say that it ain't just a lot saner, when I look at individuals who I saw nutty within the last few weeks? Ain't it a lot saner? How does it get that way? Character and responsibility. The Farm is a place to learn and to improve yourself, and the way that you improve yourself is by having this great big old rock like the Farm to push against, to try your young strength against, and see can you budge it or

 not. All we're trying to do is just turn enough beans to keep alive, and be nice and friendly to our fellow people. Nobody's making any money, nobody's getting rich.

Now the position the Farm is in now, for just a quick reading of the dashboard, is accelerating in second gear; we aren't going fast enough for the ammeter to quit reading "discharge" yet, but we're picking up, and we're coming into spring now. *If you come into spring with a wintertime attitude, it's going to be a hard summer for you, too.* But there comes a time when you have to stand up; and it comes a time to start doing something; comes a time to try; comes a time for courage, but courage is useless without something to have courage about—courage depends on a certain sort of Universe in the same way that soap depends on dirt. As Pogo Possum said, "Soap without dirt is only bad-tasting cheese."

And people say, "Man, I want to be a yogi, man I want to sit zazen, I'm going to do sesshin for six months, I want to sit zazen 'til my legs fall off; I want to stand the pain, that's what I want, to stand the pain."

"Good. How about going out and painting for the Farm?"

"Well, I, uh, that is, uh, well."

That's where commitment is at. We pretty much all hit the ball when we got here, and then we got strong enough that we took in folks that needed help, but those folks were help, too, that's a mutually interdependent thing. But then we get down to here and I think, without the spiritual part of what we're doing I don't believe that it's enough to do it. If you could do what we're doing without the spiritual part, I think there would be a lot of these all over the place—a lot of people would be very happy to go to one of these if they didn't have to get involved in no heavy religion—if it worked. You see people with ads in *The Mother Earth News* that say, "Looking for a commune, middle size, no heavy religion, no drugs."

We're trying to avoid a false convention of saying what isn't real and living what isn't real, and of not living the truth in front of you as you see it. Some people are afraid to say what's really happening because they don't want to rock the boat. I don't think that a boat is necessarily healthy if it ain't rocking; it may be becalmed. I think that, in a way, we let the Gate crew take care of the heavy work for us, and we've been so well taken care of for so long down here on the reserve, here on the reservation—we let the Gate crew keep the heavies out. I remember when this place was like Dodge City, or Tucson, Arizona, in the Old West; and it ain't anymore because we did something. Sitting around for the evening and arguing for something that you believe in is a fine thing to do; it's good to have some friends to do it with.

This is a school, and everybody came here to learn something. The reason that we are here at all is because of a body of knowledge about human relationships that we brought with us. It ain't on account of the amount of money that we brought with us. We didn't have that much money, and we were pretty poor and ignorant. We've been incredibly lucky. If we didn't have the amazing strength of being spiritual and collective, we would have been wiped out years ago. We're bad businessmen, we didn't bring a lot of skills with us, but we're really learning it, butting our heads against the brick wall. And we came with a certain set of assumptions about human relations: we said it's even worth it to go through a little hassle if you're going to get to the truth on the other end, *just as long as you get through,* not a continual low level of background noise, background radiation, click click click . . . going all the time.

We are trying to tell people what we are doing backed with our honest intelligence from the experiment at hand, not an *a priori* idea. We aren't telling them that if you chant the Bogusiddhi it will be all right. It will be all right if we truly and really understand how much we love each other, and really treat each other that way, that we love each other and really take care of all of us, and anybody else we can take care of that we are strong enough to reach.

We've made a promise by our actions to the people of the world. We've made a promise that *We ain't going to forget you*. We go into the penitentiary and say *We ain't going to forget you*, go into deep ghettos and say *We ain't going to forget you*, go down to Guatemala—*We ain't going to forget you*. And there is no Farm apart from individuals sitting here. It doesn't come in a box like a jack-in-the-box; you don't have a semi load of Farm and you unload the Farm-semi and set it up; it is not a set of Lincoln Logs. We're figuring it out as we go. I want to see value in our own revelations. I love the old books; the old books are beautiful, but I want value in our own revelations, the revelation that we share. That's what I talk about when I talk about our old hippie ways, old hippie forebears. That's sort of halfway a joke. *But this is a real revelation, and if this revelation doesn't get recognized we don't deserve revelations if we don't recognize them when they come, and we've all had revelations.* You know more about the Universe than they told you in the third grade and college and graduate school.

There's another thing that's happening in our minds and our hearts about how we are getting along together, because we are a computer, too. Just because I said, "computer," don't think that we are mechanical. We're a very Holy computer, and we are a very remarkable computer, each connection of which has free will. It is a computer with morals, because all of our intersections have "yes" and "no"—you have your yes and you have your no. And we've agreed to do this thing.

When I got really stoned, I learned what the agreement really meant, and how deep you really get into it. I saw what a lifetime agreement could look like, and I saw what a lifetime disagreement could look like.

Now I've been through a lot of changes in the time that you folks have known me—almost ten years some of you have known me—I've really been through some far-out changes, and a lot of things have gone on. And everything that I have been doing through all of those changes was following one thing, of *what is a real lifetime agreement,* what is real love, not a one-night stand, what is the definition of those kinds of things from the highest level from where they really are. I saw how strong it was, "If any two people shall agree touching anything, that shall be done"—that's from the *Bible.* And there are folks that go off of the Farm that I actually just consider that they are a Farm wherever they are. Somebody writes me a letter back from wherever they are and I say, "We have a Farm in so-and-so." because somebody that I have that agreement with is there. Sometimes I feel like people coming through the Farm are like coming through a circus tent on the trapeze and they come swinging through and you try to catch; you miss sometimes and you go, "Oops," and you go through and you hope they'll come back through on another orbit, but sometimes, . . . But sometimes, when it's really working good in the circus you hear these hands go *whack* on the wrists when they hit and you know they connected solid, and you ain't going to drop them—we have caught a lot of folks like that. But this thing here is supposed to be a giant agreement—it *is* a giant agreement, but within this agreement there are lines of trust here. I could pick out ten people that I could name right now and I could say these ten people can trust each other. You could send them off to the moon together. I ain't going to, because we have no reason to go to the moon.

What were you going to say, Gary?

"When you were talking about how we are making a dif-ference, I thought about that, and I thought that there is no Farm other than just us, and I thought that when we left San Francisco it wasn't to go get a place to be, it wasn't to go get a farm, it was to *make a difference,* and it was just us, an agree-ment of a bunch of us folks that wanted to make a difference, and that's why we are here right now is that this is what we thought was going to make the biggest difference, and if it doesn't look like it is, then we'll probably just go and do some-thing else—whatever we think is going to make a difference."

Yes, thank you for that. It's really true. We didn't leave San Francisco to go look for a place to be. We left San Francisco to make a dif-ference, and this is what we got involved in, in making a difference. Oldest perma-nent floating crap game in town. Only beatniks in the world with their own red light and siren.

I think that the weather is going to be good and that we can trust that we are going to continue to have Sundays and we don't have to do it all today. That's all we went out for was to make a difference, and we're doing it; but it's a drop in the bucket, a spit in the ocean for what we have to grow.

I love you. Good morning. God Bless you.

March 13, 1977